Help!

I'm Teaching Middle School Science

Help!

I'm Teaching Middle School Science

By C. Jill Swango
and Sally Boles Steward

NSTApress
National Science Teachers Association
Arlington, Virginia

National Science Teachers Association

Claire Reinburg, Director
J. Andrew Cocke, Associate Editor
Judy Cusick, Associate Editor
Betty Smith, Associate Editor

ART AND DESIGN Linda Olliver, Director
    Ellen Joy Sasaki, Cover and interior illustrations
PRINTING AND PRODUCTION Catherine Lorrain, Director
    Nguyet Tran, Assistant Production Manager
    Jack Parker, Electronic Prepress Technician
MARKETING Holly Hemphill, Director
NSTA WEB Tim Weber, Webmaster
SciLinks Tyson Brown, Manager
    David Anderson, Web and Development Coordinator

NATIONAL SCIENCE TEACHERS ASSOCIATION
Gerald F. Wheeler, Executive Director
David Beacom, Publisher

Help! I'm Teaching Middle School Science
    NSTA Stock Number: PB170X

    12 11 10   7 6 5

Copyright © 2003 by the National Science Teachers Association.

Library of Congress Cataloging-in-Publication Data

Swango, C. Jill, 1956-
  Help! I'm teaching middle school science / by C. Jill Swango and Sally Boles Steward.
    p. cm.
Includes bibliographical references.
    ISBN 0-87355-225-3
1. Science—Study and teaching (Middle School)—United States—Handbooks, manuals, etc. I. Steward, Sally Boles, 1973- II. Title.
    LB1585.3 .S93 2002

    507'.1'2—dc21   2002153474

    eISBN 978-1-93353-180-9

Featuring SciLinks—a new way of connecting text and the Internet. Up-to-the-minute online content, classroom ideas, and other materials are just a click away. Go to page ix to learn more about this new educational resource.

C ONTENTS

About the Authors

C. Jill Swango, an educator since 1978, has been teaching middle school science since 1986. When she first began teaching science, she had a teacher edition of the textbook and some very limited supplies—a few boxes of rocks, some test tubes, barometers, thermometers, and a compass. Jill realized it was going to take more than this to teach her subject area because she believed hands-on experiences help students understand science. So she diligently worked long hours searching for labs and finding the materials needed to perform them. Today she truly appreciates the lab classroom in her new school built six years ago and marvels at the information her fingertips can gather on the Internet. She still gets nervous, excited, anxious, and challenged every time a new school year begins. When these feelings no longer exist, Jill has decided it will be time to move on to her next daring encounter as an educator, whatever that may be.

Sally Boles Steward had the good fortune of beginning her science teaching career under the direction of her science department head, mentor, and friend Jill Swango at Brownsburg Junior High School in Brownsburg, Indiana. After a few short years teaching seventh grade science and coaching junior high and high school swimming, Sally made an unexpected, but happy, career switch and assumed the position of executive director of the Indiana Middle Level Education Association (IMLEA), the Indiana affiliate of the National Middle School Association. This position took her back to the campus of Butler University, her alma mater, where IMLEA is housed within the Butler College of Education. She enjoys working with teachers in the area of professional development and middle level best practices. Sally is also attending Indiana University School of Law–Indianapolis pursuing her Doctor of Jurisprudence. She lives in Danville, Indiana, with her husband, Matt Steward, where she enjoys spending time with family and restoring her 1840s era home.

Introduction

Help!

I'm Teaching Middle School Science was written to give you, as a new teacher, practical help on making your first year with middle school science students productive. Although the book does not place its emphasis on theory, the end of almost every chapter includes a "National Science Education Standards Note" that connects the chapter to the pertinent Standard set forth by the National Research Council in their 1996 publication *National Science Education Standards*. These end-of-chapter notes will help you become acquainted with the teaching Standards that have been espoused by the National Research Council and adopted or adapted by most states as their state standards.

Reference and resource sections are also included at the end of most chapters. The resource sections are again printed as one of the appendices so you have a quick reference list that can be readily photocopied.

SciLinks, explained below, are included for most of the chapters.

Any of the material in the book can be reproduced for purposes of classroom or workshop instruction.

How can you and your students avoid searching hundreds of science websites to locate the best sources of information on a given topic? SciLinks, created and maintained by the National Science Teachers Association (NSTA), has the answer.

In a SciLinked text, such as this one, you'll find a logo and keyword near a concept your class is studying, a URL (*www.scilinks.org*), and a keyword code. Simply go to the SciLinks website, type in the code, and receive an annotated listing of as many as 15 web pages—all of which have gone through an extensive review process conducted by a team of science educators. SciLinks is your best source of pertinent, trustworthy Internet links on subjects from astronomy to zoology.

Need more information? Take a tour—*http://www.scilinks.org/tour/*

Why Did We Write This Book?

Congratulations! You have secured a position to teach the fascinating world of science to middle school students!

Science to young adolescents!?!

Before your elation turns to hesitation, and then outright dread, know that we are here to help. Think of this book as an inanimate but spirited mentor to turn to for questions or problems as you take on this challenging, yet ultimately rewarding, task. The book is full of ideas, examples, hints, and tidbits that will help you prepare for and sail through the school year ahead. We have been in your shoes, and we only wish this help had been available in a book during the first year each of us taught middle school science.

The first thing for you to realize as a middle school science teacher is that things don't always happen the way the textbook says. Some items may not be available, some substances and supplies may not be approved for use in your school district, or the science department budget may not allow for the many instruments or equipment the teacher's manual suggests you use. Your textbook may suggest 50 minutes for a particular activity, but your class periods may be only 44 minutes. The textbook may have 25 chapters, but you may have only one semester for that subject. Obviously, you must learn to be flexible and creative when dealing with your curriculum and textbook.

The second thing to realize is that your students may come with different science backgrounds. Some will complain they "have already done this" while others will not have had many hands-on experiences and will be lost when you use common terminology—or there may be special needs students in your classroom who will pose extra challenges in making science class a worthwhile experience for them.

By this time, you should realize you must never assume anything.

Perhaps the scariest thing of all is preparing for that first day of school. What will you do? How will you open the school year in a way that builds enthusiasm for your subject and also sets the standards for appropriate and respectful behavior in your classroom for the rest of the school year?

In the pages ahead, we share some of the ice-breakers we have used on those first few days of school to build the students' enthusiasm while sneaking in some basic science class skills and expectations. Next, we become laboratory aides for you with hints and examples about everything from setting up your lab safely to assessing your students' work. Additionally, we discuss the im-portance of modeling for your students, a key to successful middle school education. Then we clue you in on reviewing or introducing measurement and the metric system in ways that will engage your students rather than frustrate them. Need to know how to make phenol red solution or inexpensive crystal growing formulas? Check out the recipe section in Appendix B. And we have a section rich in some of our favorite resources that provide additional information for the course of the school year and beyond.

Our main purpose is to get your career as a middle school science teacher off to a great start. It's up to you to go on.

We envision that you will find this book so useful you will carry it with you from home to school and back as you plan your year. Rather than write the typical instructional aid for teachers, we have left out much of the theory and tried to pack in practical ideas you can start using immediately. Use the book as a tool to help you create a classroom where your students will learn the wonders of science and be excited about coming to your class every day.

As we said, we don't want to overload you with theory, but you should become acquainted with the National Science Education Standards (NSES), established in 1996 by the National Research Council (NRC) as the basis of learning for K–12 science. Most state standards are based on the national Standards. If you aren't familiar with them or your state standards, it's a good idea to work on becoming so. This book will help: At the end of each chapter you'll find a note telling you which teaching Standards are aligned with the material in the chapter. (The full text, *National Science Education Standards* [NRC 1996] is available in hard copy, or online if you don't want to invest in the book yet.)

But our main purpose for your first—and future—years of teaching science is to help you develop a wide repertoire of teaching methods that will inspire your students to seek their own learning opportunities. That's known as inquiry, and it's a Standards-supported approach to learning that you should also increasingly be attuned to. (More about inquiry in Chapter 3.)

The NSES vision for science teaching says, "What students learn is greatly influenced by how they are taught. The decisions about content and activities that teachers make, their interactions with students, the selection of assessments, the habits of mind that teachers demonstrate and nurture among their students, and the attitudes conveyed wittingly and unwittingly all affect the knowledge, understanding, abilities, and attitudes that students develop." (NRC 1996, p. 28) We have learned that this statement could not be truer, and we hope to introduce you to some of the aspects of middle school science teaching that will help you provide your students with the best possible education.

Good luck. We'll be with you all the way.

Reference

National Research Council. 1996. *National science education standards*. Washington, DC: National Academy Press. Online version at: *www.nap.edu/books/0309053269/html/index.html*

Resources

Book/Print

American Association for the Advancement of Science (AAAS) and National Science Teachers Association (NSTA). 2001. *Atlas of science literacy (Project 2061)*. Washington, DC: AAAS and NSTA. ISBN# 0-87168-668-6

American Association for the Advancement of Science (AAAS). 1993. *Benchmarks for science literacy (Project 2061)*. Washington, DC: AAAS. ISBN# 0-19-508986-3

National Research Council. 1996. *National science education standards*. Washington, DC: National Academy Press. Online version at: *www.nap.edu/books/0309053269/html/index.html*

The First Day

ELLEN JOY SASAKI

The students' faces said it all when Mr. Juarez announced they were having a quiz. The emotions ranged from dread through irritation to disbelief.

"But you didn't tell us we were having a quiz! This isn't fair. I didn't even study! This is only the first week of school!"

Juarez quietly handed out the quiz and asked the students to begin. The room grew quiet as the students resigned themselves to the task at hand.

Before too long, he began to notice some odd looks coming from his students, questioning looks that seemed to say, "You've got to be kidding." He simply looked away.

Then, one by one, students began rising from their seats, circling their desks, shouting out their names, and mooing like cows. Giggles came from the other students who didn't read quite as fast. But when they got to the same items on their quizzes, they got up and mooed too.

Finally, as they reached the last item, students gasped, then laughed, and knew they'd been had. "Now that you've read all 10 items as instructed in item 1, go back to the beginning and respond only to item 2," it said.

Oh yes, it is important to read all the directions before you begin working!

You have your materials all ready for the first day: classroom roster, seating chart—filled out and seats assigned, textbooks to distribute, bus forms, cafeteria forms, student forms, teacher forms, office forms, parent forms, discipline program forms, and checklists to account for all the forms sent out, filled out, and collected. Your classroom rules, lab safety rules, team rules, homework policy, and grading policy are hole-punched and ready to share with your class. You have more than 200 note cards ready for students to give you information for your personal file. Whew! This scenario will occur in most classes the student has that first, important day of school.

Not the way you envisioned setting the classroom tone for the rest of the year, but what choice do you have? How about some ideas, games, and activities that will captivate students' enthusiasm for science and problem solving?

First pass out all the forms that must be filled out or sent home that day with any necessary instructions and distribute the textbooks to ensure there are enough for all students, telling them to keep these in their lockers for the next couple of

days. Then begin teaching science skills, but in a rather sneaky, entertaining way. There are many, many teaching tools out there—in kits, online, and from a variety of books and magazines. They include board games, crossword puzzles, tangrams, word games, and brainteasers. They are wonderful teaching tools for problem solving, problem finding, cooperative learning, and communication skills.

Icebreaker activities, such as the one that starts this chapter, can begin the school year while giving students a chance to get acquainted. We've listed 10 icebreakers that can be used the first few days to introduce problem solving to your students and establish a sense of classroom community.

1. Tell Me About Yourself

Stand outside the classroom door and greet each student with a roll of two-ply toilet paper, directing students to take as many sheets as they need. Some students will take one sheet, and some will attempt to take the entire roll, so have an extra roll, just like you would at home. Some students will look at you strangely or ask a question or two. Just repeat the instructions to these apprehensive and curious pupils. Other counting items besides

SCiLINKS®
THE WORLD'S A CLICK AWAY
Topic: new teacher resources
Go to: www.scilinks.org
Code: HMS06

toilet paper squares can be used, of course, but the look on students' faces when they are greeted with toilet paper is worth experiencing.

Once class has started and all the necessary business has been completed, ask students to separate the sheets into individual squares. Instruct students who take only one or two sheets to separate the plies.

Inform students that the number of sheets or plies they have is equal to the number of things they must share about themselves with the class. As students react to the instructions, it is particularly entertaining to see the expression of those who took nearly half a roll. But when it comes time for the students to speak, tell them they have to share only a maximum of five things about themselves. That gets the activity completed in a timely manner and earns gratitude right from the start from the students who took a lot of paper.

After the activity, explain how important knowing one's colleagues is to establishing rapport and good working relationships. You probably will have a chance right then to increase the students' vocabularies by defining—and perhaps even spelling—the word "rapport."

2. The Simplest Quiz

Many of the questions you will need for "The Simplest Quiz" can be found online. (See Resources.) Tell students you are curious about the things they know and that this short quiz will help you determine what items need to be reviewed. Distribute the quiz. Here are some sample questions:
• How long did the Hundred Years' War last?

• What was King George VI's first name?
• How long did the Thirty Years' War last?
While walking around the room as they take the quiz, mention that you are not sure whether to record their quiz grades. Expect a fair number of students to practically beg you to put this in the grade book.

When finished, let your students grade their own quizzes and then go over the answers as well as explanations:
• 116 years, from 1337 to 1453.
• Albert. When he came to the throne in 1936 he respected the wish of Queen Victoria that no future king should ever be called Albert.
• 30 years, of course!
No matter how many questions are on the quiz, always end with the Thirty Years' War.

This quiz demonstrates that everything is not always what it seems. (See also Icebreaker Number 6.) Explain to your students that, in science, some explanations or theories may be hard to understand or even see, but they are the best answers we have for now. You can stress the importance of hypotheses, observations, predictions, and inferences in scientific study by using this activity.

3. A Picture Is Worth Several Words

Another concept using puzzles to illustrate looking at things differently is called word pictures. Word pictures are fun, and many students have already been exposed to this type of puzzle. These puzzles have a box with letters and/or symbols arranged to represent familiar phrases or sayings. For example,

Figure 2.1

(three blind mice)

(no U turn)   (I understand)

After this activity is completed, remind students that many scientific discoveries occurred because someone looked at an event or problem differently than anyone ever had—for instance, Newton and gravity, Archimedes and buoyancy, Wegener and plate tectonics. (See Resources.)

4. "Equations"

Another fun puzzle that helps students think differently involves symbols, abbreviations, and equations. (See Resources.)

Ask the students to complete the following equations:

- 36 = I. in a Y.
  (36 = Inches in a Yard)
- 7 = Y. of B. L. for B. a M.
  (7 = Years of Bad Luck for Breaking a Mirror)
- 2,000 = P. in a T.
  (2,000 = Pounds in a Ton)
- 3 = S. Y. O. at the O. B. G.
  (3 = Strikes You're Out at the Old Ball Game)

5. Don't Forget the Details

To illustrate to students the importance of listening to every detail and making logical inferences, try reading them a scenario and challenging them to guess what is happening in a given situation. For example:

A man went out for a walk. While he was walking, it began to rain. He was not wearing a coat or hat, and did not have an umbrella. He continued to walk. His clothes and shoes got wet, but his hair did not. Why?

You may need to read the story again before you ask for student responses: The answer is that the man is bald. This usually brings moans and groans, but students are always willing to hear another. (See Resources.)

6. Things Aren't Always What They Seem

An entertaining way to illustrate the importance of observation skills is to use images that create optical illusions. You can find them online, in books, and on cards. Making transparencies to be viewed on the overhead is one way of showing them to your class. Or they can be scanned and shared through media retrieval processes. Here is a very simple optical illusion:

Which inner circle is smaller?

Figure 2.2

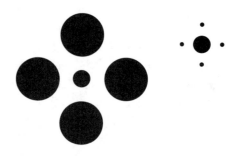

Look closely, they are the same size.

Any of artist M. C. Escher's works—which can be found in poster and prints, and in book— have excellent visual properties. Students who can see all aspects of these special pictures can help students having problems discerning the differences.

Don't be surprised if your students continue finding and copying different visual illusions for you throughout the year. Make a habit of displaying them so others can enjoy them, too. These pictures can be wonderful sources for cooperative group learning or peer teaching as well. (See Resources.)

7. Outside the Box

Another important part of science is thinking outside the box. Most students have heard this before, and the following posers help demonstrate the meaning of the phrase. (See Resources.)

Question: I have 55 cents. I have two coins in my hand, and one of them is not a nickel. What coins do I have? **Answer:** A 50-cent piece and a nickel. The 50-cent piece is not a nickel, but the other coin is.

Question: The doctor gives me three pills and tells me to take one every half-hour. How long does it take to use up the pills? **Answer:** One hour. Take pill one; take pill two a half-hour later; take pill three after another half-hour.

Puzzle: Connect the dots using four straight lines without lifting your pencil from the paper:

Figure 2.3

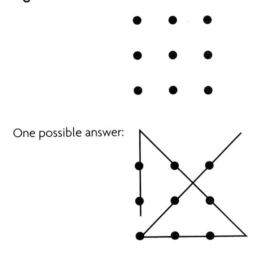

One possible answer:

8. Survival—Marooned on the Moon

This is an activity that places students in a situation requiring decisions about survival. Based on an exercise developed by the National Aeronautics and Space Administration (NASA), the website describes a catastrophic scenario on the Moon and lists material to be ranked in order of importance for survival. First, each student ranks the items. Next, a small group rehashes their rankings, and then the entire class works together to reach a consensus. They can compare their answers and their reasoning to NASA's analysis. This activity reinforces one of the basics of lab work. Even though students' measurements and observations differ slightly when they are working through an experiment or hands-on activity in class, the students as a whole need to come to the same basic conclusion.

9. Just Read the Directions

This skill emphasizes following directions, in the same way the vignette at the beginning of this chapter did. From Appendix A, photocopy "Can You Follow Directions?" on page 92. This is a long list of instructions, the most important being item number one, "Read everything carefully before doing anything," and the last item, "Now that you have finished reading everything carefully, do only sentences one and two."

A few students will carefully follow the directions, or will have seen this exercise, but some students will race through the directions because it is a timed test. The discussion the class has after this activity will reveal that all the students can remember a time they wished they had read the directions for a task before beginning. Several of these tests are floating in cyberspace waiting to be downloaded, but you can also add your own mischievous directions.

10. Name That Object

The following three exercises will help students develop lab skills.

• Select 15 or so pieces of lab equipment used throughout the year, separate them into three or more areas around the room, and number them. Give the students a list of the devices' names and challenge them to match the items with the names using the numbers as references. After an allotted amount of time has passed, ei-

ther go over the answers or tell the students you have planted the answers somewhere around the room. Good places are under lab areas or student desks, on the goggles cabinet, and near the eye wash station.

- Depending on the number of students, number of specimens, and available classroom space, set out several identical groups of rocks, then have student groups sort the rocks according to characteristics the teacher, class, or group selects. Have magnifying glasses, water, scrap paper, streak plates/tile pieces, and any other types of testing materials available at each area. After an allotted time, have student groups travel to the different areas to compare their rock classifications with others, then discuss the techniques used to sort the different rocks.

- Display three items that might not seem connected in any way, such as a lightbulb, a beaker of salt water, and a blown-up balloon. Have the students list numbers one through four on the paper, then roam around the room and fill the blanks with the names of four different students in the class. Instruct students to make sure their student lists match up; for example, if Sy has Carol listed as number one on his sheet, then Carol should have Sy's name as number one on her sheet. It may be necessary for you to fill in for a student, depending on number in the class. Then call out one of the four numbers—in order or randomly—and have the students who have that number meet. Tell them to discuss the characteristics and uses of one of the items for an allotted time. Repeat the process two more times. For the last group, tell the students to decide how the items are connected in science. In the example of the lightbulb, balloon, and salt water, electricity would be a possible answer. Have the last student group write their names and answers on a piece of paper, and then collect the papers. Have the groups share with the class their answers and explanations with the class.

Icebreakers Work All Year

There are other ways to start the school year, but icebreakers can be most successful. They help create a comfortable, lively, and active atmosphere students will come to expect and enjoy when they enter. Don't limit yourself to using these types of activities only at the beginning of the year. Use them also to rejuvenate after a long break, after a long, difficult unit has been covered, or before beginning a new unit. Students will understand the reasons for group work, perk up when it comes time to problem solve, and be able to help each other "see" other methods or answers to problems. And, when your students go home after those first days of school, your class will be the one they talk about at the dinner table.

Resources

Periodicals

Games Magazine, PO Box 2055, Marion, OH 43306-8155 (puzzles and games)
World of Puzzles (by Games Magazine), PO Box 2032, Marion, OH 43306-8132 (puzzles and games)

Web Source URLs

Please note that websites are often changed, deleted, and moved.

Website	Subject
www.wpafb.af.mil/cap/glr-ae/lplan/oct96.htm	survival
www.geocities.com/vishalmamania/jokes/quiz.html	simplest quiz
www.norfacad.pvt.k12.va.us/puzzles/wacky.htm	word pictures
www.halcyon.com/doug/ucg/kids/riddles.html	word pictures
www.mcps.k12.md.us/schools/tildenms/Departments/ P.E/SmithStuff/wacky_wordies.htm	word pictures
webhome.idirect.com/~avriljohn/visual.html	visual illusions
www.cs.brandeis.edu/~hornby/amuse/test_mental.txt	equations test
kith.org/logos/things/sitpuz/situations.html	situations
webusers.anet-stl.com/~kveit/me00002.htm	posers
www.thewaitegroup.com/jokes/j54.html	posers
www.elseroad.com/fun/intelligence/intelligence_test.htm	posers
www.dorsai.org/~walts/iq_test.html	posers

National Science Education Standards Note:

*This chapter specifically addresses Teaching Standard A, bullet point two, and Teaching Standard B, bullet points two, four, and five.

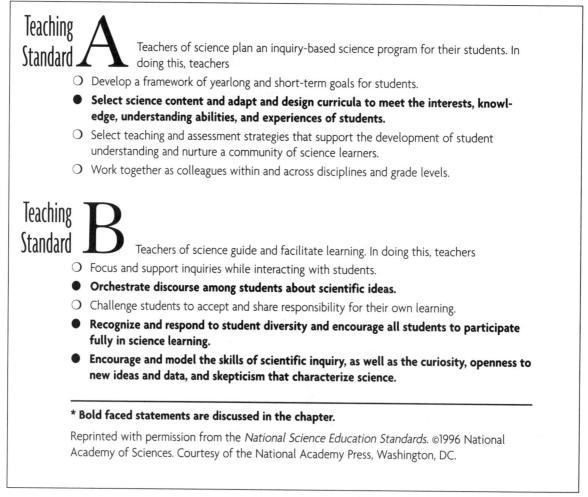

Teaching Standard A

Teachers of science plan an inquiry-based science program for their students. In doing this, teachers

○ Develop a framework of yearlong and short-term goals for students.

● **Select science content and adapt and design curricula to meet the interests, knowledge, understanding abilities, and experiences of students.**

○ Select teaching and assessment strategies that support the development of student understanding and nurture a community of science learners.

○ Work together as colleagues within and across disciplines and grade levels.

Teaching Standard B

Teachers of science guide and facilitate learning. In doing this, teachers

○ Focus and support inquiries while interacting with students.

● **Orchestrate discourse among students about scientific ideas.**

○ Challenge students to accept and share responsibility for their own learning.

● **Recognize and respond to student diversity and encourage all students to participate fully in science learning.**

● **Encourage and model the skills of scientific inquiry, as well as the curiosity, openness to new ideas and data, and skepticism that characterize science.**

* Bold faced statements are discussed in the chapter.

Reprinted with permission from the *National Science Education Standards.* ©1996 National Academy of Sciences. Courtesy of the National Academy Press, Washington, DC.

Best Practices

Front-page articles in science and education periodicals and journals give voice to the growing concern that scores on nationwide science exams have either declined or, at best, have had a minute increase even after several years of pushing for better science learning. With this reality facing science education, being knowledgeable about some best practices in science instruction is important.

Developmental Needs of Young Adolescents

When discussing best practices, it is imperative, first, that you understand the developmental needs of your students. Unfortunately, many educators try to teach young adolescents as if they are just big elementary schoolers or little high schoolers. Of course, neither is true. Middle school students are unique individuals with specific needs educators must meet if they are going to help them achieve their fullest potential. The Center for Early Adolescence at the University of North Carolina at Chapel Hill has determined seven specific developmental needs of young adolescents that must be met in our schools and classrooms if we are going to tap into our students' potentials. The National Middle School Association endorses these needs:

Physical Activity—Because this period of life is one of rapid growth and change, students must be given opportunities to move around frequently to alleviate stress on growing bodies.

Competence and Achievement—Adolescence is a period of acute insecurity. Seeking out and rec-ognizing students' achievements helps them maintain a positive self-image.

Self-definition—For perhaps the first time in their lives, students are starting to test their wings. Giving them opportunities for different learning experiences helps them define who they will become in adulthood.

Creative Expression—Young adolescents seek out ways to express the new feelings and thoughts they are experiencing. Providing opportunities for project-based learning and artistic expression in your science classroom will tap into this need and open doors your students never knew existed.

Positive Social Interaction with Peers and Adults—Young adolescents have an intense desire to be with others and to try out their social wings. Structured interaction within your classroom allows them not only to be social with you and other students but also to enhance their own learning and that of others. (See Chapter 5: Cooperative Learning and Assessment.)

Structure and Clear Limits—Although young adolescents may tell you they want more freedom, they still have a childlike need to know the boundaries that keep them safe from harm. (See Chapter 10: Classroom Management.)

Meaningful Participation—Everyone needs to feel needed. During a tumultuous developmental period of life, participation becomes even more important. Providing your students with opportunities to be meaningful contributors in their schools and communities promotes good citizenship that will carry over into adulthood.

Learn the Techniques

Before deciding on some best practice techniques to use in the classroom, consult the school district curriculum, the state standards, and the National Science Education Standards (Remember these from Chapter 1?). Another resource is the *Atlas of Science Literacy* (AAAS and NSTA 2001), a publication that is part of the American Association for the Advancement of Science's Project 2061, a long-term effort to improve science, math, and technology education for grades K–12. The *Atlas* uses strand maps built from national benchmarks and learning goals to represent graphically the importance of vertical articulation and progression in science by connecting the ideas and skills learned from kindergarten up through grade 12. It presents a framework to coordinate science, math, and technology and can be used with different instructional strategies.

Inquiry

From the perspective of inquiry-oriented instruction, learning is an active process in which students develop new ideas or concepts based upon their current understanding. The role of the teacher changes from providing information and answers to structuring activities that challenge students' awareness and comprehension of science. There are different methods of inquiry a teacher can draw from:

Topic: science as inquiry
Go to: *www.scilinks.org*
Code: HMS13

Structured—Students are provided with a problem and procedures but not the outcome. The students develop concepts of relationships between variables during the investigation.

Guided—Students are provided with the problem and materials but come up with their own procedures to solve the problem.

Open—Students formulate the problem to solve as well as the procedures that will solve the problem.

Learning Cycle—Teacher leads student through guided inquiry and discussion. Students then apply what they have learned to a new situation.

The teacher facilitates learning as a type of coach, moving among groups and asking questions that guide students toward the conceptual objectives. Thus the goals of inquiry in science instruction are a more student-centered process, hands-on experiences, and ample time to explore and learn about science interactions and concepts (Colburn 2000).

Modeling

But young adolescents also need direction. You can accomplish this through modeling, which provides instruction, builds important skills, and gives students a point of reference for all types of classroom lessons and assignments. (See Chapter 8 for a detailed discussion of modeling.) Modeling is just what it implies: showing your students all the steps they need to complete a task, whether it be written work, lab experiments, note taking, or group projects.

Modeling eliminates confusion over a teacher's expectations. Studies in adolescent development have shown it is normal for adolescents to become insecure and upset when they do not feel in control of their surroundings or themselves. If they do not know what "to do," tension and uneasiness may replace open-mindedness and critical thought. That means your lesson may be lost if you do not model the appropriate methods for your class before the task begins. Modeling shows students step by step what is expected of them,

giving them control and security to think about the task and concepts at hand (Holliday 2001a).

Scaffolding

Scaffolding is an instructional procedure related to modeling. Just as a scaffold is a supportive, but temporary framework for concrete objects, this technique gives support through coaching and modeling and is relinquished as students acquire mastery levels. Scaffolding is task oriented and works well with science lessons incorporating technology. Teachers can scaffold by providing prompts, links, and guides in an active learning environment that eventually leads to student self-reliance (Holliday 2001b).

A big part of the scaffolding process is cooperative learning. Cooperative learning involves students working together to attain a common goal. The keys to using cooperative learning are structuring the activity so the success of the entire group depends on the interaction of its members, perhaps by rotating role assignments, and making sure the assessment measures the individual's and group's achievements, using tools such as self-evaluations and checklists. You may find it necessary to help students develop interpersonal skills and effective group dynamics at first, but the social skills rewards gained through positive interdependence, interaction, and processing are worth the practice time (Holliday 2001b).

Project-Based Learning

The goal of the next best practice, project-based learning, is providing opportunities for students to find solutions evidenced in end products of their own designs. Each project has a focus that will involve inquiry, problem-solving techniques, and student or group products—artistic, dramatic, musical, construction, for instance—that can be used for assessment. Students collaborate, sharing and presenting information and products and using technology to access the information. They can also help you with objectives, planning activities, and evaluation. These processes encourage inquiry, aimed at engaging and enhancing a student's higher order thinking skills. Students gain self-confidence and become more motivated learners, and teachers get solid evidence of student accomplishment. The active involvement of students in project-based learning helps them see a purpose in learning, and the end product can give them a real sense of achievement and closure (Ediger 2001).

Hands-On

These best practices all hinge on hands-on activities. Science textbooks, science resource books and periodicals, science education websites, and science conferences and workshops offer a multitude of labs, activities, and demonstrations that cover the realms of science study. Many of the materials you need can be purchased through science catalogs or even at your grocery, drug, or hardware stores. If you have enough funding, you can also use science kits specifically developed for teaching a certain science concept or entire unit. Many of these include much of the material you will need for a classroom of 20 to 30 students as well as guidelines and timelines. There are also materials for event-based science series and programs such as the online Jason Project that are real-life and real-time science. Activities and the materials needed to complete them are relatively accessible, but deciding how best to teach the science behind them revolves around awareness, research, and decision. (See Resources for information on these materials and programs.)

References

American Association for the Advancement of Science (AAAS) and National Science Teachers Association (NSTA). 2001. *Atlas of science literacy (Project 2061)*. Washington, DC: AAAS and NSTA. ISBN# 0-87168-668-6

Center for Early Adolescence. 1985. *Seven developmental needs of young adolescents*. Carrboro, NC: University of North Carolina at Chapel Hill.

Colburn, A. 2000. An inquiry primer. *Science Scope* 23 (6): 42–44.

Ediger, M. 2001. A project method in middle school science. *IN Focus* 30 (Summer): 17–19.

Holliday, W. 2001a. Modeling in science. *Science Scope* 25 (2): 56–59.

Holliday, W. 2001b. Scaffolding in science. *Science Scope* 25 (1): 68–71.

Resources

Web Source URLs

Please note that websites are often changed, deleted, and moved.

Website	Subject
www.weather.com	The Weather Channel
spacelink.nasa.gov/index.html	Spacelink resources for educators
www.nasm.edu	National Air and Space Museum homepage
www.middleweb.com	middle grades instructional methods and resources
www.physics4kids.com	teacher and student information
www.biology4kids.com	teacher and student information
www.chem4kids.com/	teacher and student information
school.discovery.com/lessonplans/index.html	lesson plans
www.pacificnet.net/~mandel/index.html	lesson plans
scifun.chem.wisc.edu/	lesson plans
scssi.scetv.org/cgi-bin/state/indxsrch?q_f=15	lesson plans
www.teach-nology.com/teachers/lesson_plans/science/basic	lesson plans
www.exploratorium.edu	museum site
www.project2061.org	Benchmarks search engine, online guides, ordering, information
www.youth.net/nsrc	inquiry and kit-based science education
www.ces.clemson.edu	inquiry and kit-based science education
www.si.edu/nsrc/laser/overv.htm	inquiry and kit-based science education
einsteinproject.org	inquiry and kit-based science education
www.jasonproject.org/	live, interactive programs
earthobservatory.nasa.gov/Laboratory/	event-based inquiry experiments
www.pearsonlearning.com/dalesey/full_event.cfm	event-based inquiry titles

Book/Print Sources

American Association for the Advancement of Science (AAAS) and National Science Teachers Association (NSTA). 2001. *Atlas of science literacy (Project 2061)*. Washington, DC: AAAS and NSTA. ISBN# 0-87168-668-6

American Association for the Advancement of Science (AAAS). 1993. *Benchmarks for science literacy (Project 2061)*. Washington, DC: AAAS. ISBN# 0-19-508986-3

Center for Early Adolescence. 1985. *Seven developmental needs of young adolescents*. Carrboro, NC: University of North Carolina at Chapel Hill.

Connors, N. A. 2000. *If you don't feed the teachers they eat the students! Guide to success for administrators and teachers*. Nashville, TN: Incentive Publications, Inc. ISBN# 0-86530-457-2 (humorous advice for educators)

Irvin, J. L., ed. 1992. *Transforming middle level education: Perspectives and possibilities*. Boston: Allyn & Bacon. ISBN# 0-205-13472-6

Rutherford, F. J., and A. Ahlgren. 1990. *Science for all Americans*. New York: Oxford Press. ISBN# 0-19-506771-1

Schurr, S. L. 1998. *Dynamite in the classroom: A how-to handbook for teachers*. Westerville, OH: NMSA Publications. ISBN# 1-56090-044-5 (middle grades instructional methods)

Wormeli, R. 2001. *Meet me in the middle*. Westerville, OH: Stenhouse Publishers in conjunction with the National Middle School Association. ISBN# 1-57110-328-7 (middle grades instructional methods)

National Science Education Standards Note:

*This chapter specifically addresses Teaching Standard A, bullet points two and three, and Teaching Standard B, bullet-points one, four, and five.

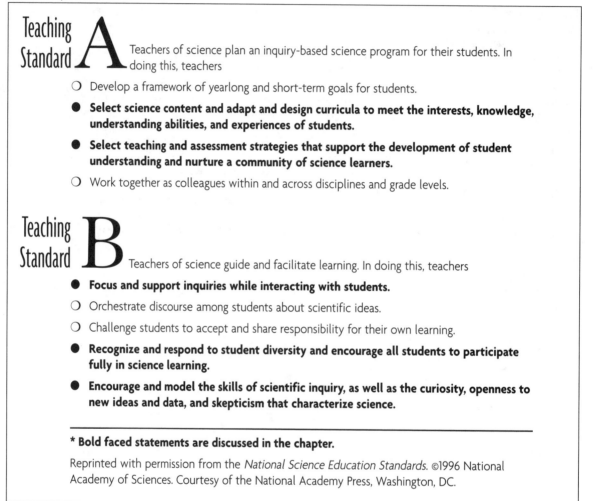

Teaching Standard A Teachers of science plan an inquiry-based science program for their students. In doing this, teachers

○ Develop a framework of yearlong and short-term goals for students.

● **Select science content and adapt and design curricula to meet the interests, knowledge, understanding abilities, and experiences of students.**

● **Select teaching and assessment strategies that support the development of student understanding and nurture a community of science learners.**

○ Work together as colleagues within and across disciplines and grade levels.

Teaching Standard B Teachers of science guide and facilitate learning. In doing this, teachers

● **Focus and support inquiries while interacting with students.**

○ Orchestrate discourse among students about scientific ideas.

○ Challenge students to accept and share responsibility for their own learning.

● **Recognize and respond to student diversity and encourage all students to participate fully in science learning.**

● **Encourage and model the skills of scientific inquiry, as well as the curiosity, openness to new ideas and data, and skepticism that characterize science.**

* Bold faced statements are discussed in the chapter.

Reprinted with permission from the *National Science Education Standards*. ©1996 National Academy of Sciences. Courtesy of the National Academy Press, Washington, DC.

Lab Set-Up and Safety

Ms. Malloy opens her classroom door for the first time, flips on the light, and takes a tentative look inside her domain. A certain thrill races through her body, just as it did when she was told she had secured this job. The task of decorating and arranging the space bounded by these four corners instantly presents itself, and Malloy begins to take stock of what is there. Of course, there are some questions: Is this room to be shared with others? Is it used solely for science purposes? How many

students are in the largest class? Are there enough desks, tables, and chairs?
These are indeed important issues, with answers dependent upon personal
choices or hurdles of each situation. However, Malloy can begin to plan for
the set-up and safety issues that take place in what she hopes will be the
busiest learning area of the room, the lab.

Whether your assigned classroom is for science labs or there is a specific science lab area shared among several teachers, you need to set up properly for group experiments and other hands-on activities. There are several ways to set up lab groups in various combinations, depending upon class size, available materials, and storage space. Some schools have spacious rooms with desks and lab areas that include cabinets, sinks, and an adjoining teacher prep/storage room, while others may have one sink, little storage space, and desks or tables with stools or chairs.

SCI*LINKS*
THE WORLD'S A CLICK AWAY
Topic: safety in the
science laboratory
Go to: *www.scilinks.org*
Code: HMS20

Getting Supplied

You can arrange lab groups by pulling desks or tables together for whatever size group you need—small groups of two to three or large groups of five to six students. For storage space, consider asking if the department or school has funds to purchase some plastic storage carts, stackable bins, or freestanding standing shelves units. If money is tight, ask the custodians, teachers, administrators, and other staff members in the building or school district if these types of items are in storage or not being used. Try contacting local businesses or parents, too—by newsletter, during open house or conference days, or through parent support groups at school. When

these appeals reap rewards, write down the items and the donor so you can send thank-you notes. The Flinn Scientific catalog is one source for help on the mechanics of setup. Before long, your science room/lab area will have storage areas just ready to be stocked. Also, be sure to check science supply catalogs for kit-based science (see Resources). Kits provide all the materials you need for an entire classroom about a specific unit of study. If your school doesn't already cut costs by purchasing one classroom set of textbooks rather than individual books for each child, you might want to ask it to do so. This frees up money that can be spent on other needed materials and resources.

This, of course, brings up the issue of equipment. You must survey and inventory the lab supplies available: chemicals (dispose safely of any leftover chemicals); substances; glassware; hardware; software; lab equipment (pulleys, pH meter, and rock samples, for example); instruments such as microscopes, stopwatches, and thermometers; textbooks; teacher resources; and cleaning supplies, among other items. Use this inventory to start three lists for purchases: items needed immediately, items needed within a grading period, and items needed for the semester. Also, make a wish list of items to purchase over the course of two or three years. (See Resources for a list of science supply companies.)

A middle school usually has more than one science lab area to be equipped, and budget constraints may not allow for all to be outfitted properly right away. Many items may have to be shared, but they can last for a long time if they are cared for properly. A cart on wheels is useful for taking supplies and equipment from room to room or, if you are sharing a room, for keeping everyone's supplies and equipment separate. Be responsible by cleaning up lab and prep areas, washing lab dishes and supplies, and putting away materials and supplies in a timely manner for others who may need them. There may be separate accounts for items that fall under book rental, student fees, or school district resources. If so, record the items appropriately on the account register.

Get your lists to the person responsible for purchasing department supplies as soon as possible. Be descriptive in the requests, noting the item size and amount, or including catalog pages, item numbers, and prices, if applicable. Not only will you receive exactly what you wanted, but it is also a courtesy to the person doing the ordering and purchasing, who will be very grateful.

Usually, even on a shoestring budget, lab supplies can be procured. Here are some suggestions:

- Instead of ordering chemicals, check to see if common materials can be substituted. (See Resources.) Some labs call for simple household substances, and you can buy these cheaper, and with no shipping fees, from local grocery, department, or drug stores.
- Contact local pharmacies, chemical companies, other businesses, and universities to see if they ever give away or donate used lab equipment. See if the high school science department has any supplies that could be borrowed or given away. Make certain that donated equipment includes no old chemicals: You will be responsible for their safe disposal.

- Grants are available that may include funds for needed supplies. (See Chapter 11 Resources for information about grants and grant writing.)
- Check with parents, school staff, and parent groups for items that could be used as substitutes in the lab, such as baby food jars, one- and two-liter bottles, wire, wood scraps for ramps and other items, nuts and bolts, tweezers, matches, measuring cups, utensils, clamp clothespins for test tube holders, and funnels, which also can be made by cutting off the top part of liter bottles.
- Check out local garage sales, or generate a materials list and give it to people who thrive on going to garage sales.
- Check out exhibits and exchanges at museums, fairs, science conventions and expositions where rock samples, fossil casts, guidebooks, and other such items are available.

Be creative, and do not be afraid to ask.

To show appreciation, take pictures of the students using the supplies or equipment and send them to the local newspaper or school newsletter with a list of donors, or send the photos to donors to include in company newsletters, bulletin boards, or flyers. Be sure to check with your administrators about the proper procedure for publishing student likenesses and names. Letters of thanks from you and your students are also a good idea.

Put Safety First

Student safety is your job number one. Safety in the lab begins at once and with proper equipment. It is the rule and the primary objective in the science classroom. Materials and equipment must be properly maintained, arranged, and stored in the manufacturer's suggested way. Many science supply companies that sell chemicals not only list codes for safety but also give out guidebooks for storage and removal. Make sure you know your school's policies for these.

There should be a flammables cabinet and acid cabinet with key lock or padlock in the science classroom, storage room, or department office for potentially dangerous substances. Never leave these items out overnight, and keep them within your awareness or your reach throughout the day if they are being used. Check to see if your school has a hazardous chemical/materials policy. If any of these items are in the storage area, contact the proper person to get them out. When purchasing a chemical, check in the science supply company catalog to see what type of shelf life it has. Buy only what you need for the year. Label the purchase year on chemical bottles and containers—companies that supply chemicals for schools often will do this for you. If there are any chemicals or materials in an unlabeled bottle, notify the proper person get them out as soon as possible. There should be a material safety and data sheet (MSDS) file on hand for each chemical stored in an area. These sheets, which contain pertinent information about the chemical, come with the chemical or can be accessed through the Web or by a letter of request (See Resources).

You must have several pieces of safety equipment for experiments:

- A fire extinguisher and a fire blanket, necessary for activities using open fire.
- An eye wash station, although you can demonstrate chemicals with only a sink available for an eye wash if you are willing to risk your own eyes.
- A fan/exhaust or fume hood system for any experiment that produces smoke or fumes. Any kind of smoke can produce asthmatic attacks.

Proximity to a shower area is also a necessity. Many such showers have an eye wash station attached to them. While we are on this subject, know that an eye wash station must either be hooked up to a faucet or have a full reservoir of water imme-diately available upon a push of a lever or pull of a cover. The eye wash station must have water gushing out from two opposite points to hit both eyes and the face. If the eye wash station consists of a squirt bottle used by covering one eye at a time, tell the department chair or an administrator that the liability associated with the responsibility of helping a student decide which eye to save in an accident is something you do not want to face. And you might not save even one because squirt bottles don't hold enough water to irrigate the eyes. If you can't get an adequate eye wash, you may want to demonstrate yourself, or even omit, any lab that requires hazardous material.

Know where to find the emergency turn-off button or handle for electricity, gas, or water. Make sure there is proper cleaning equipment for spills or breakage.

There should be goggles approved by the American National Standards Institute (ANSI) and aprons for each student. If chemicals are going to be used, chemical splash goggles are best. Goggles need to be cleaned after student use. A germicidal goggles cabinet, if the lab has one, can fill this bill. If not, you can dunk the goggles into a container of diluted antibacterial cleaner, rinse them off, and then dry them. Some teachers have used germicidal gel to clean goggles, but check to see if the manufacturer approves its use. Even if you have a germicidal cabinet, you may want to clean goggles every now and then with antibacterial cleaners. If chemicals or combustibles are going to be used primarily in lab, the lab aprons should be the rubberized types or those noted as flame retardant. Aprons should be cleaned occasionally by rinsing them off and hanging them up separately to dry.

There should be chemical spill gloves available for students as well as heat-protective gloves, grippers, or potholders.

You should have a healthy supply of rubber bands for students with long hair to use on lab days, especially if they are using combustibles. Students using the rubber bands can throw them away when the lab is completed.

Train Students

It is imperative that students know you are very serious about lab safety. Take students on a "field trip" to the storage area and show them the flammables and acid cabinets, how the chemicals are stored, and the MSDS file. Remind them they are not to go into the storage area without a teacher. There are a couple of lab demonstrations you can use to show students the importance of goggles and in using care when working with flammables, but do not use alcohol burners because they are very flammable and easy to knock over. (See Flinn Scientific website in Resources.) Show students where all the safety equipment is housed and how it is used. Have a student demonstrate using the eye wash station; let each student try out the goggles, aprons, and gloves; and remind them of the "stop, drop, and roll" move.

Give each student a lab safety rules sheet, and send a copy home to parents. Another copy should be posted in the room. (See Appendix A, p. 93 for sample or the Flinn Scientific website in Resources). Take the time to go over the rules, making sure students understand what is expected of them. Keep emphasizing to students that safety is very important and that any violations may result in serious consequences and then tell them what the penalties are (see Appendix A, p. 94, for laboratory tickets). Many science safety seminars suggest students sign a safety contract with parent signature also required (see Flinn Scientific website in Resources) and pass a lab safety quiz before being allowed to take part in the first lab (See Appendix A, p. 95, for sample quiz).

If you plan to make the first lab one no student will want to miss—anything involving fire makes most middle school students drool uncontrollably—many students will make it a point to pass that lab safety quiz on the first attempt. If a student does not pass the test, then he or she should do seat work or a worksheet that corresponds to the lab. Students who do not pass should be given another opportunity to pass a different lab safety quiz. If this does not do the trick, a quick call home may help, but the student should continue to do seatwork instead of lab work until the requirement is met.

One last point about student lab safety: Never let students perform a lab you have not tried first—without exceptions even for labs that look harmless. Life has surprises enough, why tempt more? If you are familiar with the experiment of the day, the result will be better student understanding and more teacher satisfaction—and your students will be safer.

Labs need your full consideration because they are an integral part—sometimes the most important part— of a student's science learning experience. Your and your students' respect for and attention to safety issues are absolute necessities.

Resources

Science Supply Companies

Many of these companies offer kit-based science resources. Chemicals purchased from many of these companies will include the MSDS.

AIMS Education Foundation, PO Box 8120, Fresno, CA 93747-8120
1-888-733-2467 (*www.AIMSedu.com*)
Carolina Biological Supply, 2700 York Road, Burlington, NC 27215
1-800-334-5551 (*www.carolina.com*)
Flinn Scientific, Inc., PO Box 219, Batavia, IL 60510
1-800-452-1261 (*www.flinnsci.com*) This company catalog lists chemical storage and removal guidelines.

Frey Scientific, 100 Paragon Parkway, PO Box 8108, Mansfield, OH 44903
1-800-225-FREY (*www.freyscientific.co*m)
Nasco, 901 Janesville Ave., PO Box 901, Fort Atkinson WI 53538-0901
1-800-558-9595 (*www.eNASCO.com*)
Pitsco, Inc. PO Box 1708, Pittsburg, KS 66762
1-800-358-4983 (*www.shop-pitsco.com*)
Sargent-Welch/Cenco, PO Box 5229, Buffalo Grove, IL 60089-5229
1-800-727-4368 (*www.sargentwelch.com*)
Science Kit & Boreal Laboratories, 777 East Park Drive, PO Box 5003, Tonawanda, NY 14151-5003
1-800-828-7777 (*www.sciencekit.com*)

These companies sell small toys and other items that can be used in hands-on activities:

Oriental Trading Company, Inc., PO Box 2308, Omaha, NE 68103-2308
(*www.orientaltradingcompany.com*)
US Toys Co., Inc., 13210 Arrington Road, Grandview, MO 64030-2886
Mindware, 121 5th Avenue NW, New Brighton, MN 55112
(*www.mindwareonline.com*)

Book/Print

Kwan, T., and J. Texley. In press. *Inquiring safely: A guide for middle school teachers.* Arlington, VA: NSTA Press.

Web Source URLs

Please note that websites are often changed, deleted, and moved.

Website	Subject
physchem.ox.ac.uk/MSDS/	MSDS information
www.msdssearch.com/	MSDS information
www.ilpi.com/msds/index.html	MSDS information
quizhub.com/quiz/f-chemicals.cfm	common chemical names quizzes
chemfinder.cambridgesoft.com/	common chemical names database

National Science Education Standards Note:

*This chapter specifically addresses Teaching Standard D, bullet points two, three, and four.

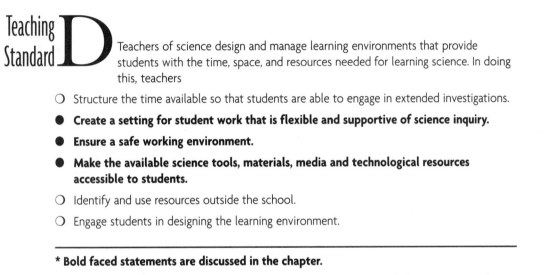

Teaching Standard **D** Teachers of science design and manage learning environments that provide students with the time, space, and resources needed for learning science. In doing this, teachers

○ Structure the time available so that students are able to engage in extended investigations.

● **Create a setting for student work that is flexible and supportive of science inquiry.**

● **Ensure a safe working environment.**

● **Make the available science tools, materials, media and technological resources accessible to students.**

○ Identify and use resources outside the school.

○ Engage students in designing the learning environment.

---

* Bold faced statements are discussed in the chapter.

Reprinted with permission from the *National Science Education Standards.* ©1996 National Academy of Sciences. Courtesy of the National Academy Press, Washington, DC.

Cooperative Learning and Assessment

ELLEN JOY SASAKI

"Can we do this with partners?" says the class social butterfly.

He always wants to work with a partner, but this time other students chime in their agreement with his request.

Ms. Sanders ponders a moment. She quickly thinks through the assignment and decides partners would be appropriate, with some minor adjustments.

"Certainly, but with some requirements. First, let me remind you that, when we work with others, it is so we can help each other learn even more than we could by ourselves. Second, working with others does not mean one person works and the other sits."

The students nod; this is a mantra they have heard all year.

Sanders then assigns specific roles and responsibilities for each partner to be sure everyone is pulling his or her weight and the concepts to be learned are not lost in the social aspects of group work. She makes it clear each student will be responsible for producing his or her own written work.

While the students pair off and get to work, she moves around the room to help less socially developed students find a partner and then to make sure the groups are on task.

Every expert you consult will tell you that, to successfully teach science to your students, you must include numerous hands-on activities that encourage inquiry-based learning, opportunities for simulation exercises, freedom to explore and discover, and laboratory exercises that bring textbook lessons to life. However, what many experts may not warn you about are the logistical challenges that come along with an active science classroom. When addressing perhaps the two most challenging aspects of your lesson planning you may catch yourself having this conversation with yourself:

"I don't have the budget or space to let each child work through this project as an individual. How should I group the students so I know everyone will have the chance to participate and learn as much as they can?"

If you manage the grouping, the conversation will probably continue in this direction:

"Once I do have the students grouped, how do I assess them so each individual is graded on his or her effort and not the efforts—or lack thereof—of the group as a whole?"

Not all teachers face these challenges so frequently. The other "core subject" teachers in your building most likely do a great deal less project-based learning. However, the art of grouping and assessment in an active science classroom comes down to a little common sense and an old adage: Variety is the spice of life.

Variety is also the key to successfully grouping and assessing your students. In the next few pages we look at the definition and purpose of cooperative learning, strategies for grouping your students, three proven methods for assessing your students' collaborative efforts individually and in groups, and, finally, how all this affects special needs students.

SCI**LINKS**
THE WORLD'S A CLICK AWAY

Topic: assessment strategies
Go to: www.scilinks.org
Code: HMS28

What Is Cooperative Learning?

Cooperative learning in its simplest sense is two or more students working together on an assignment. In an expanded definition, cooperative learning becomes an opportunity for students to interact with one another intellectually and socially under the guidance of the teacher. It allows students to work together toward common goals, beneficial for all learners within the group. (Johnson, Johnson, and Holubec 1994). At its best, cooperative learning allows the teacher to become the "facilitator of learning" while the students, with the help of one another, become the directors of their own discovery and learning process.

Advantages of Cooperative Learning

Research has shown that students in a cooperative learning setting score higher on achievement tests than those who learn by other methods (Wood 1992). But perhaps an even more important advantage to cooperative learning methods is the intellectual and social interaction it allows your students. The Center for Early Adolescence at the University of North Carolina at Chapel Hill (1985) cites "positive social interaction with adults and peers" as one of the seven key developmental needs of young adolescents (See Chapter 3, p. 13, for the list.). Science and psychology has taught us that, developmentally, young adolescents need opportunities for social interaction in a meaningful way in order to develop into healthy adults who can interact positively with society. Listed in the table below are some of the other advantages of cooperative learning.

Disadvantages of Cooperative Learning

In a well-organized classroom, there are only two disadvantages to cooperative learning, and both can be remedied with some common sense and by using the tips from this chapter on assessment methods.

The first disadvantage is that of the "lazy student" or the "know-it-all student." We all have both of them, and we all want to scream sometimes when we think of the waste of talent the lazy student can be or the overbearing annoyance the know-it-all can be. People who oppose cooperative learning—unfortunately, often the parents of your "overachiever" students—will tell you that the bulk of the cooperative learning

---

TABLE

5.1

Other Advantages of Cooperative Learning

- Students of higher ability who work with students of lower ability develop empathy and "people skills" while assisting classmates.

- Students of lower ability who work with students of higher ability are given the chance to be part of a successful academic endeavor, thus increasing their confidence level.

- Groups of students who work together will often bounce ideas and questions off one another, and their collective imagination can lead to further questioning and to more discovery of knowledge.

- From a strictly financial standpoint, cooperative learning requires fewer materials than individual work and can save money for a strained science department budget.

work in a group will be done by a few hardworking students or one know-it-all, while the remaining students will ride on their coattails and miss out on the learning opportunity.

The second disadvantage is the question of how to assess group work. Those same critics who are worried one student will do the work for the group will pose the question, "Why is it fair to give the kid who did nothing the same grade as the kid who did everything?"

The answer you should give to both questions is "Cooperative learning doesn't work that way in my classroom." In the next few pages we will show you ways to make sure each member of your cooperative learning groups plays a role and ways to individually assess a student for work done in a group. And you'll learn how to back up your answer to critics' objections.

Great Grouping Methods

Although cooperative learning is much more than just putting students together and telling them to get to work, sometimes the hardest part for a new teacher is how to group the students. Several methods for determining groups follow. In addition to forming groups, you should assign students specific roles—one role to a student—that allow them to track their group's progress and assist you in managing their own progress (Lanzoni 1997) . According to Lanzoni, some suggested roles for students are

- Director (aka Spokesperson, Manager, Presenter, Leader)
- Writer (aka Scribe, Secretary, Record Keeper)
- Checker (aka Foreperson, Procurer, Materials Manager)
- Assistant (aka Helper, Facilitator, Arranger, Inquiry Person)

It is important that you define the roles clearly so each student knows what you expect and what

you will be using for assessment. Once roles have been determined and defined, you are ready to group your students. Some of the methods below can help you get started.

Random Selection

This method is not only the easiest for you, but also the hardest for students to complain about.

When to Use: Use this method for short projects, one or two days at the most. This method is good for assignments that are related to the textbook or that have very specific easy-to-follow instructions.

How to Group: Decide on a category, such as birth months or people who are wearing red. Continue to break groups down by random characteristics until you have the group size you want. You can also have students choose numbers or names out of a hat and match their numbers or names with each other, or use a similar drawing. You can always rely on the physical education teacher's old standby and have your students count off by twos, threes, fours, or however many groups you want.

Advantages: This method is quick and requires little planning. Additionally, it gives students the opportunity to work with any of their classmates, thus increasing their interaction with one another, and discourages group reliance on one classmate because students have no idea whom they will end up with.

Disadvantages: You can't control who works with whom. You need to either let the students know you have veto power over the random outcome or take your chances on whatever groups you get—hence, the suggestion this method be used only for short assignments. It is better to allow the groups to stand as drawn, but if you end up with a truly terrible group, don't be afraid to tweak with a "teacher veto."

Grouping by Strengths

This method requires quite a bit of work on your part prior to starting a project, but usually results in well-balanced groups that can work together and successfully complete the assignment.

When to Use: This method is best for the more complicated and lengthy projects.

How to Group: Determine the most appropriate size of group for the project. Get out your class roster, and start placing students into groups based on their strengths. Start by placing a student with good leadership qualities into each group. Move on to those students who have good organizational skills. Then look for students who follow directions well. Then place students who work well with others. When you come to the end of the list, you will probably have only a few students who don't exhibit one of these strengths or another strength you determine is useful. Those challenging students should then be spread among the groups. When you tell the students their group assignments, do not get into a discussion about your methods, but posting groups on a bulletin board may help alleviate their curiosity. If they ask, you can answer, "I just made sure there were the right number of people in each group and there were no bad combinations."

Advantages: This method allows you to make sure each group has at least a couple of members who will stay on task and focused, which should help the group as a whole. It also gives you the power to make sure no bad combinations happen.

Disadvantages: Young adolescents realize quickly why certain students were placed in a certain group. If you use this method more than once during a school year, you must be careful to mix up the students so they do not feel you have labeled them. And remember, young adolescents change from day to day; your born leader today may be your tongue-tied follower tomorrow.

The Dreaded Coed Grouping

Use this method if you've got the sense of humor and patience to witness adolescence at its best—or worst!—while encouraging positive academic interaction among the sexes.

When to Use: Although you may want to avoid it, girls and boys do need to learn to work together, and middle school is the time to start learning. This method is good for short assignments that require conversation and discussion and can be completed by groups of two, three, or four.

How to Group: You can allow students to choose their own coed groups, or you can go the random drawing route if you are concerned that some "wallflowers" may be left out.

Advantages: This grouping method forces your students to learn to work with members of the opposite sex in an academic setting. Many of your students will also be on their best behavior for this assignment because they will be trying so hard to impress their group members.

Disadvantages: The newness of working with someone of the opposite sex may be overwhelming for some of your students. So overwhelming, in fact, they may not be able to concentrate on the task at hand until they get used to this grouping. Make sure the first assignment you give in this situation is a simple one, or a review, so even students who are distracted can successfully complete the assignment. Although some students may behave better to impress group members, others may misbehave to impress their group members. This method requires you to be on your toes and ready to redirect group activity if it gets off track. However, using it once in a while helps your students

develop social skill. And, you will find, the students will adjust to interacting with each other and you will be able to expand on the complexity of the projects as the school year passes.

Student Choice

Your students will love the opportunity to pick their own groups, but beware of the pitfalls of this method and use it sparingly.

When to Use: You are the only one who can decide if a particular class is mature enough to choose to work with people who will not distract them or cause them to behave in a manner counterproductive to the task you have assigned. Additionally, use this method only if your class is compassionate enough to make sure every student is invited to be in a group. If you are unsure, you may want to make some of the stipulations listed further on.

How to Group: If you have a perfectly well-mannered, mature class you can allow your students to choose their own groups based on the group size you dictate. However, most classes of middle schoolers are not perfect. The best way to account for your students' shortcomings, while still allowing them the freedom to choose their own partners, is to stipulate the makeup of the group before they choose. Tell them "Your group must have at least two boys and two girls" or "Your group must include at least one person who was born in September, October, or November." Think creatively about other ways to define the groups, and you'll avoid some of the disadvantages listed below.

Advantages: Students this age love to be with their friends, and their happiness level will never be higher in your classroom than when you let them choose their own groups. Also, many of them are sharp enough to realize they must choose partners wisely if they are to complete your assignment successfully. With some guidance from you, your students will learn the fine art of decision making and may even start to learn how important an influence their choice of friends has on success.

Disadvantages: Every classroom has its share of loners, troublemakers, and painfully shy students. They are not likely to be chosen first when you allow students to choose their own groups. That is why you must carefully stipulate how groups are chosen so everyone is needed to fulfill group requirements. Try to steer your loners and shy students toward groups where you know the other students are compassionate and friendly. Try to steer troublemakers toward groups where the students are confident and capable and not easily swayed by mischief. While groups are being chosen, you should be making sure everyone is finding a place.

Ability Grouping

Unless your administration has given you prior approval, grouping students by academic ability within the same classroom should probably be avoided. If you are planning a complex project and want to make different assignments to each group based on individual expectations, you could consider grouping by ability. Make sure you consult your administration first to discuss your project and plans.

Lab Partners

Some science teachers like to assign permanent lab partners as in a collegiate level course. Although this method works well in college, it is not appropriate developmentally for middle school children. Young adolescents need to learn to work with all types of people, and they need you to provide—even force them into—situations in which they can interact with students of differing abilities, personalities, and backgrounds.

TABLE
5.2

The Science Teacher's Rules of Grouping

1. Make sure each student has a role to play in the group. (See Chapter 10: "Classroom Management.")

2. If the students are choosing/finding group partners, put a short time limit on the time they have to find a group. Thirty seconds is plenty of time. If they don't have a group by then, place them yourself.

3. Make sure <u>each</u> student has a copy of directions to refer to, whether on a handout you give them or written on the overhead or the board.

4. Place time limits on the tasks you want the groups to accomplish. This will help them stay on schedule and not get sidetracked with socializing.

5. "Float" around the room during group work to provide guidance, answer questions, and keep groups focused on the assignment.

6. If the assignment and groups are for more than one day, write down the names of the members of the group so no one can "forget" the next day.

7. Don't forget to include the names of absent students in groups that will work more than one day together.

8. Group work must stay in the classroom.

The Next Step ... Assessment

Although cooperative learning is a wonderful tool in the science classroom, it does require you be more creative when assessing your students' work on labs or projects. Giving a standard pen-and-paper test based on project or lab work may not be a logical method of assessing knowledge. In order to ensure students are graded based on their own individual learning, as well as the group's work as a whole, you will need to use several methods of assessment. Three key methods are rubrics, teacher observation, and student evaluations.

Rubrics

A rubric tells students what you expect from them in a project. You design it before assigning a project and give it to the students to refer to while they are working on the assignment. When you design your rubric, set up the learning expectations for a project, establish point values for superior, good, average, and unsatisfactory work for each expectation, and then briefly describe for the student what each of those expectations is for each point value.

The rubric for a project where students create a solar system model might look like Table 5.3.

You should include all the expectations you have for a project as well as any work habit expectations you have for the student. The key to success in using rubrics is to make sure you define your expectations clearly and provide your students a copy of the rubric before they begin working so they can keep those expectations in mind throughout the process. Rubrics are an excellent way to help your students develop the ability to monitor their own learning processes and accomplishments while providing you with an accurate assessment of group work. A "fill-in-the-blank" sample rubric is provided for you in the Appendix A (p. 97) to help you get started using rubrics.

Teacher Observation

As students work on projects and labs, you, no doubt, will be floating around the room, providing assistance, answering questions, and keeping groups focused on their task. While you are doing this, you can also be assessing each student's work. It is helpful to carry a class roster with blank lines by each name. As you work your way around the room, note what you see students doing, questions you hear them asking, and successes you see them making. Of course, if you see them misbehaving, off task, or otherwise not assisting the group, note this as well. Note the time of each observation on your roster. Later, when filling out

---

TABLE 5.3

Solar System Model Rubric

Assignment Due Date:_____ Student Name:_____

Expectations, Descriptions, and Point Values

1. All nine planets and the Sun are represented accurately.

    ● **4 points-Superior** (Planets are sized realistically to one another. Planets are spaced realistically to one another. Color is used to show characteristics of the planets. Motion of the planets is modeled.)

    ● **3 points-Good** (Planets are sized realistically to one another. Color is used to show characteristics of the planets. Motion of the planets is modeled.)

    ● **2 points-Average** (Color is used to show characteristics of the planets. All planets are present and in proper order.)

    ● **0–1 points-Unsatisfactory** (None of the above has been achieved.)

2. The finished product is neat and of high quality.

    ● **4 points-Superior** (Work is of excellent quality and is extremely neat.)

    ● **3 points-Good** (Work is of good quality and is mostly neat.)

    ● **2 points-Average** (Work is of satisfactory quality and is somewhat neat.)

    ● **0–1 points-Unsatisfactory** (None of the above)

Total Points Possible: 8   Total Points Earned:_____

Comments: _____

the rubrics for each student, you can consult your observations sheet to add to the "Comments" section. You can use your observations to determine at what level each student met the assignment. Having your observations written down on paper for them to see and noting the time tells your students you are aware of their individual efforts and that those efforts have a direct effect on the grade they receive. These comments also can come in handy during parent-teacher conferences.

Student Evaluation

At the conclusion of a group project, but before assigning final individual grades, it is a good idea to get some feedback from your students about how they felt their groups worked together to make sure you didn't miss anything during your classroom observations. One easy-to-administer method could proceed as follows. Ask students to

- Take out a sheet of paper and write the names of their group partners, leaving two or three spaces between each name. Make sure they list themselves last.
- List the biggest contribution each member made.
- List one way each member could improve for the next project.
- Rate their group members on a scale of 1 to 5. Explain in detail your expectations for each numeric value, and give them examples.
- List their own contribution, how they could improve, and a self-rating.

When you collect the evaluations, be sure to keep the comments and ratings to yourself. You can read the comments and average the ratings to determine how each member performed. That will help you determine an appropriate grade for each group member. If you have a student consistently struggling to work as part of a group, sharing these comments confidentially during a student-teacher conference or a parent-teacher conference can be helpful. Students who have extreme difficulty working in groups might be candidates for a referral to your school's guidance counselor. Then the comments you collect from peers, as well as your observation log, can serve as background information for the counselor.

Be warned: You will find, more often than not, young adolescents are much harder on themselves than you might expect, but they are quite forgiving of one another. Keep that in mind as you read these evaluations. Still, the comments the students make should shed light on what really happened during the group work process.

Special Needs Students

Special needs students require special care, but whatever kind of special need a student has, be sure you let your special education colleagues know your lesson plans and ask for their help in adapting your plans to meet the needs of the students. Special education teachers can let you know what expectations are reasonable and how you can adapt your lessons to provide an equitable learning environment for all your students.

Behavior/Emotional Issues

Project work can be a problem for students with behavioral concerns. Many emotionally challenged students and students have issues working and communicating well with others. Although it is important to provide them with opportunities to learn how to interact with others, it is also important to ensure your special needs students do not completely disrupt the learning process for the rest of the class. You must walk a fine line to accomplish this.

If you have the luxury of a teacher's aide in the classroom, be sure the aide stays with the student at all times to make sure he or she is focused on

the learning task and is not disrupting the group's progress. If the student cannot work in a group without unreasonable disruption, it may be necessary to provide a version of the project for the student to do alone, or, if you are doing a lab, you may need to provide a separate lab set-up for the student to complete with the teacher's aide as partner. Sometimes, another student who has proved to work well with special needs students and is capable of directing the learning process can act as a "peer tutor" partner.

Physical and Mental Disabilities

You should modify group work for students with physical disabilities just as you would for their other activities. Prior to the assignment, think through possible stumbling blocks and determine the best way to reduce or eliminate them.

Students with mental disabilities can be integral parts of a group project at their own ability level. When making an assignment, think of tasks at that student's level and make sure the group knows those tasks are the responsibility of the special needs student. For example, if your groups are making models of the solar system, a severely mentally disabled student could be responsible for coloring the Sun or one of the planets under the tutelage of the other group members. During labs, simple tasks that teach direction following and sequencing could be the responsibility of students with mental disabilities. They may do a good job of getting supplies out and ready for each step or cleaning up the lab area.

ESL Students

You will need to consult with the English as a second language (ESL) teacher about the language level of ESL students before you can determine what roles these students can play during cooperative learning. Many times, simply being part of the group and having the opportunity to listen to native speakers of English will be an asset for students just acquiring the language.

Learn More

Once you master the fine art of grouping and assessment, planning for project-based learning and hands-on lab activities will be much easier. Use a variety of techniques and a little common sense and you'll be on your way to creating an active and involved learning environment. Because cooperative learning should be such a large part of your teaching and learning methods, we recommend you take the time to read up on cooperative learning to expand your abilities in this area. Some references are suggested here.

References

Center for Early Adolescence. 1985. *Seven developmental needs of young adolescents.* Carrboro, NC: University of North Carolina at Chapel Hill.

Johnson, D. W., R. T. Johnson, and E. J. Holubec. 1994. *The new circles of learning: Cooperation in the classroom and school.* Alexandria, VA: Association for Supervision and Curriculum Development.

Lanzoni, M. 1997. *A middle school teacher's guide to cooperative learning.* Topsfield, MA: New England League of Middle Schools.

Wood, K. 1992. Meeting the needs of young adolescents through cooperative learning. In *Transforming middle level education,* ed., J. L. Irvin. 314–335. Boston: Allyn & Bacon.

Web Source URLs

Please note that websites are often changed, deleted, and moved.

Website	Subject
rubistar.4teachers.org	rubrics to create online

National Science Education Standards Note:

*This chapter specifically addresses Teaching Standard B, bullet points two, three, and four; Teaching Standard C, bullet points one, three, and five; and Teaching Standard E, bullet points two, three, and four.

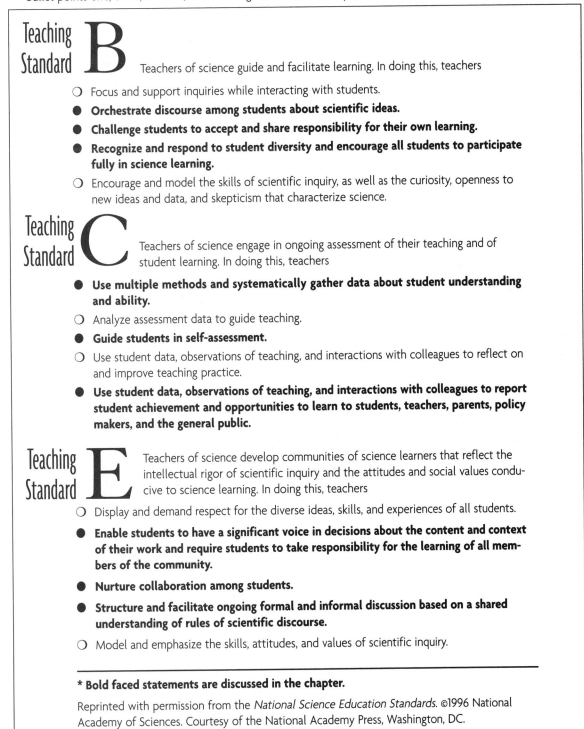

Teaching Standard B

Teachers of science guide and facilitate learning. In doing this, teachers

○ Focus and support inquiries while interacting with students.

● **Orchestrate discourse among students about scientific ideas.**

● **Challenge students to accept and share responsibility for their own learning.**

● **Recognize and respond to student diversity and encourage all students to participate fully in science learning.**

○ Encourage and model the skills of scientific inquiry, as well as the curiosity, openness to new ideas and data, and skepticism that characterize science.

Teaching Standard C

Teachers of science engage in ongoing assessment of their teaching and of student learning. In doing this, teachers

● **Use multiple methods and systematically gather data about student understanding and ability.**

○ Analyze assessment data to guide teaching.

● **Guide students in self-assessment.**

○ Use student data, observations of teaching, and interactions with colleagues to reflect on and improve teaching practice.

● **Use student data, observations of teaching, and interactions with colleagues to report student achievement and opportunities to learn to students, teachers, parents, policy makers, and the general public.**

Teaching Standard E

Teachers of science develop communities of science learners that reflect the intellectual rigor of scientific inquiry and the attitudes and social values conducive to science learning. In doing this, teachers

○ Display and demand respect for the diverse ideas, skills, and experiences of all students.

● **Enable students to have a significant voice in decisions about the content and context of their work and require students to take responsibility for the learning of all members of the community.**

● **Nurture collaboration among students.**

● **Structure and facilitate ongoing formal and informal discussion based on a shared understanding of rules of scientific discourse.**

○ Model and emphasize the skills, attitudes, and values of scientific inquiry.

* Bold faced statements are discussed in the chapter.

Reprinted with permission from the *National Science Education Standards.* ©1996 National Academy of Sciences. Courtesy of the National Academy Press, Washington, DC.

Writing for Science

Mr. Washington heard the groans as soon as he gave the assignment.

"Do we have to write complete sentences?"

"A paragraph is how many sentences?"

"You want this paper to be how long?"

And the biggest groan of all, "What does all this writing have to do with science, anyway?"

Writing, as we all know, is an integral part of any discipline. And, because of the important role that writing up lab reports and research plays in the field of science, you must help your students work on writing throughout the year.

In this chapter, we cover basic skills and methods of instruction for teaching your students proper formatting for lab reports, essay and short-answer questions, and research assignments.

The Student's Perspective

Once again, remember your students may come to you on the first day of school with a wide variety of experiences and skills from elementary school and previous middle grades. Some may be proficient writers, able to produce a two-to-three page paper on a given topic with no trouble. Others may struggle to form a grammatically correct sentence and shudder at your insistence that a paragraph *is* longer than three sentences. And it is likely none of your students, regardless of their previous knowledge of writing, will have done much writing specifically related to science class.

Before you feel overwhelmed and discouraged, think of it this way: Your students are clean slates when it comes to writing scientifically. No bad habits to break, no preconceived notions to dispel.

Topic: science writers
Go to: *www.scilinks.org*
Code: HMS40

Presenting Writing to Your Students

Most middle school kids are desperate to be grown up, or at least to be treated like they are grown up. You can use this desire to help create a positive writing experience in your classroom. When the time comes within the first few weeks of school to start that first writing project, perhaps a lab report or a research paper, drag out some of your old college lab notebooks or papers from the basement and bring them into class—only the A's and B's, of course. Let your students look at them, touch them, and read through them. Tell them that, in college, a large part of your science classes centered on writing up lab reports and producing well-written research papers that explained your topic clearly. Then announce to your students you have decided that you will teach them how to write up lab reports and papers just like college students and real scientists do. Although some of your students may go wide-eyed at this announcement, you'll notice they will begin to smile, sit up a little straighter, and lean toward you to hear just how you're going to do *that*.

Don't panic. You are going to teach them how to write up lab reports or research papers just as in college or the science research world, only on a smaller scale—which your students don't need to know at this point. Just the mere thought they are doing something a college student or real scientist might be doing that very day will hold the attention of most of the young adolescents in your classroom, at least long enough to present your case and get them started.

Three major aspects of written expression should be included in your middle grades science classroom: formal lab reports, essay and short-answer questions, and research and theme papers.

Formal Lab Reports

We all remember our lab notebooks from college science classes. They had to be meticulously kept in form, format, and content. The emphasis placed on those lab reports is key to what you should be introducing to your students. As with any assignment, your method of introduction and explanation is important.

Purpose. The purpose of a lab report is this: repeatability. Your students will understand better the reasoning behind learning how to write up a

lab report if you tell them the real-world purpose. Explain it to your students by posing the following question.

"Let's say you are a world-famous cancer researcher. You have been running a very complicated experiment for many, many months, even years, and when you come to the end you realize you've found the cure for cancer. You run down the hall to gather all the other scientists in your lab to show them the wonderful discovery you've made. When all the other scientists gather around your experiment, what do you think they will ask you?"

Answers will include: "What is the cure?" "How'd you do it?" "What did you use?" "How can we repeat it?"

Now, ask your students how they, as famous cancer-researcher scientists, could answer those questions. The answer, of course, is by referring to what they had written.

What would happen if the experiment weren't written down? It couldn't be checked. The purpose of a formal lab report is to be sure any scientist in any part of the world can take another scientist's lab report, place it in front of him or her, and repeat the experiment exactly. That is how great discoveries are proved to be more than just a fluke and how advances are made in research and technology.

Format. Most scientists use a version similar to the format below. Be sure to address the purpose of each part and explain to the students how each part relates to the scientific method. (See Appendix A [p. 98] for a reproducible version you can give students as a reference.)

- Heading—Name of student, date(s) of experiment, location
- Purpose/Objective—In one or two sentences, students answer the question, "What am I trying to learn from doing this experiment?" The answer can be in the form of a question.

- Prediction/Hypothesis—Students make a prediction on the outcome of the experiment, based on testable variables.
- Materials Needed—Students list all materials used. Explain the importance of being specific. For example, list a "500 ml beaker" instead of just a "beaker."
- Procedure—Students write out the steps they will follow to carry out the experiment. Although the steps do not have to be in complete sentences, they should be complete enough that another person could follow them exactly.
- Data Collected/Observations—Students record any measurements taken, as well as any observations they make. You will have to give clear instructions about what you expect to be included in this section .
- Charts/Graphs—If your students create any charts or graphs, they should be included here.
- Conclusion—Students write a paragraph explaining the outcome of the experiment, what they learned from it, and whether or not their initial prediction or hypothesis was right or wrong. They could also include information from their text or research that supports their conclusion.

Method for Teaching. Make sure you go over the lab report format with your students and address each section carefully. When making lab report assignments, start out slowly. For the first several labs, provide students with a handout that includes the objective, materials needed, and procedure. Ask them to write up the other sections. Once they have had a chance to see several examples of work from you, they will be ready to try their own full lab reports. Choose a simple experiment with a limited number of materials and only a few steps for their first attempt. You'll find that, by the end of the year, your students will be very adept at putting together lab reports that would make your Chemistry 101 professors proud.

Before You Start. The following advice will further help you with success in the lab.

- Requiring students to complete formal lab reports for every lab they do is not necessary. Lab reports are well suited for activities in which the outcome is not obvious and in which students have to make measurements and observations to draw conclusions.

- At least twice a year, take your students to the computer lab and ask them to type up their lab reports. Your students will see the importance of lab reports and realize just how much work they have put into an experiment. Don't forget to emphasize good spelling, punctuation, and grammar. This aspect of the process could even be done as a partnership between you and the language arts teacher.

- Collaborate with your technology teacher when doing formal lab reports. Your technology teacher can teach your students how to create graphs and charts on the computer that can be inserted into a typed-up lab report. Most word processing and spreadsheet programs come with graphing capabilities that will help your students understand the relationship between their science experiment and mathematical explanations.

Formal lab reports are a good way to help special needs students stay on task and focused. The emphasis on format and repeatability helps students who struggle with organization and following directions because the expectations and method are the same every time, regardless of the experiment itself.

Essay and Short-Answer Questions

Most standardized tests our students take now include an essay question or short-answer question that requires them to write not only for mechanics but also content.

Middle school students learn best if they are given clear steps to follow in a process. Essay questions and short answers can be taught in a step-by-step process. As with lab reports, start out at the beginning of the year with simple questions and work your way to more complicated, critical-thinking questions toward the end of the year. Here is a five-step suggestion you can pass on to your students:

- Read the whole question straight through at least once, twice, if you need to.

- Think, "What is the question here?" Underline it. Example: <u>Why is Earth the terrestrial planet best suited for human life?</u>

- Your first sentence should be a statement that answers the question clearly and concisely but without great detail. Example: Earth is best suited for human life because of unique characteristics that make it different from the other three terrestrial planets.

- Your next three to four sentences should give details that back up or provide evidence that proves your first sentence was correct. Example: The temperature on Earth is not too hot, like Venus or Mercury, and not too cold, like Mars, for humans to survive. Unlike the other three terrestrial planets, Earth has an atmosphere that contains oxygen, which humans need to live. Humans need water to survive, and Earth is the only planet that has water we can drink.

- Your last one or two sentences should restate your first sentence and wrap up the details you provided. Example: In conclusion, because of its unique temperature, atmosphere, and water, Earth is the best planet to sustain human life.

To answer short questions follow steps 1 through 3 from the preceding list.

There are differences between essay and short-answer questions. Correct answers to an essay question show evidence of enduring understanding; effective organization of written material is

part of the assessment. For a short-answer question, the focus is solely on addressing the essential question regarding a concept.

As the author of the essay questions and short-answer questions your students will encounter, you must write questions that are clear and to the point. Nothing will frustrate you or your students more than ambiguous or hard-to-understand questions. As you hone your question-writing skills, consult the questions provided with your textbooks for ideas, keeping in mind that, many times, textbook tests and assessments are not written for the reading comprehension level of your student population. Ask your colleagues to read your questions and tell you if they understand what you are asking. If they can determine your purpose, even without being in your classroom everyday, your students are also likely to understand what you are asking.

Research and Theme Papers

Research assignments are a necessary tool to help students learn how to formulate questions and search out their own answers. The research itself familiarizes students with the vast number of resources found in libraries and online, but it can be a frustrating and overwhelming task many students dread. With some simple modifications, you can help alleviate any tension the "R" word brings to your students, and open up the whole world of discoveries just waiting to be found. Don't forget—your best resource may be the language arts department in your school. Read on to learn how to help your students enjoy and benefit from their research experiences.

Provide parameters, but allow for choice. Whenever you assign a research project, you should allow students to choose their own topics within your broad guidelines. For example, if you want the students to do a research paper on plants, as-

sign the students a type of plant, say flowers or trees, but allow them to choose the species. Unless you know for sure the resources on a given topic are terribly limited, allow students to research their first choices. Giving students a choice of topic ensures their interest will last longer and they will put forth more effort.

Allow both print and electronic resources. The Internet is an invaluable research tool. If you have Internet capabilities at your school, you need to teach your students how to do a proper search— enlist the help of your media specialist or technology teacher—and how to find and cite authoritative information on the Web. The Internet is here to stay, and all your students will have to be Web-knowledgeable in whatever occupations they end up pursuing. Now is the time to start teaching them Internet basics and protocol.

If you are worried about students getting into inappropriate sites, you can limit the search engines they are allowed to use to those that are child-friendly or you can learn how to set up a Web quest for your students. A Web quest is a series of previewed websites that you program for your students to visit. They can click into and among your approved websites but cannot go outside this closed world you have created. If you need help in determining which search engines are appropriate for children, or how to set up a Web quest, schedule an appointment with your school's media specialist.

Consider assigning research projects as group or partner assignments. When you think about it, most real-world research is not the product of one person but rather of a team of scientists collaborating. Assigning a topic to groups or partners can result in students' learning about delegation of responsibility and teamwork as well as content. Divide the research assignment into parts so each team member has a specific role to play. For ex-

ample, if your students are doing a research assignment about a type of animal, divide the research into habitats, physiology and anatomy, climate, life cycle, and interesting trivia. As long as each student is responsible for a part of the whole assignment, you can be sure no one will end up doing all the work. (See Chapter 5 for more tips on group projects and assessment.)

Allow for multiple forms of presentation. Although writing will have to be involved in any way your students present their research, there is no good reason they have to write up a five-paragraph theme paper every time you assign a research project. Remember, young adolescents need variety in their lives and in their schoolwork—and so do the teachers who grade them.

Some examples of alternatives to the five-paragraph theme paper are

- PowerPoint presentations on the computer
- Posters
- Speeches
- Brochures or informational pamphlets
- Children's storybooks or flip-up books
- Videotaped presentations
- Plays or skits
- Songs/Raps/Poems
- Web pages

The possibilities for presentation of research materials are endless. The most important thing to remember is not to limit your students, or yourself, to only one form of communication. Using multiple forms of presentation will allow all types of learners in your classroom to excel at one point or another during the year.

Writing in the science classroom is a requirement, not an option. By showing your students the writing you require is something that real scientists do, by providing clear and consistent instructions about how to tackle a writing assignment, and by including a variety of instructional methods, those groans you heard on the first day of a writing assignment will turn to confident statements of "Yeah, I can do that. No problem!"

Resources

Web Source URLs

Please note that websites are often changed, deleted, and moved.

Website	Subject
www.seaworld.org	animal information database
www.yahoo.com/Education/	
www.infoseek.com	good search engine for students

National Science Education Standards Note:

*This chapter specifically addresses Teaching Standard A, bullet points two and four; Teaching Standard B, bullet points two, three, four, and five; and Teaching Standard C, bullet point one; Teaching Standard D, bullet points one, two, five, and six; and Teaching Standard E, bullet points two, three, and five.

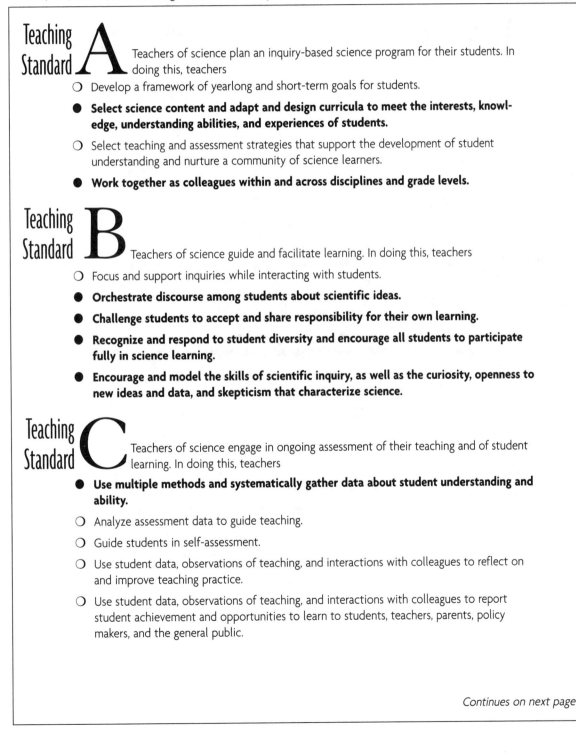

Teaching Standard A

Teachers of science plan an inquiry-based science program for their students. In doing this, teachers

○ Develop a framework of yearlong and short-term goals for students.

● **Select science content and adapt and design curricula to meet the interests, knowledge, understanding abilities, and experiences of students.**

○ Select teaching and assessment strategies that support the development of student understanding and nurture a community of science learners.

● **Work together as colleagues within and across disciplines and grade levels.**

Teaching Standard B

Teachers of science guide and facilitate learning. In doing this, teachers

○ Focus and support inquiries while interacting with students.

● **Orchestrate discourse among students about scientific ideas.**

● **Challenge students to accept and share responsibility for their own learning.**

● **Recognize and respond to student diversity and encourage all students to participate fully in science learning.**

● **Encourage and model the skills of scientific inquiry, as well as the curiosity, openness to new ideas and data, and skepticism that characterize science.**

Teaching Standard C

Teachers of science engage in ongoing assessment of their teaching and of student learning. In doing this, teachers

● **Use multiple methods and systematically gather data about student understanding and ability.**

○ Analyze assessment data to guide teaching.

○ Guide students in self-assessment.

○ Use student data, observations of teaching, and interactions with colleagues to reflect on and improve teaching practice.

○ Use student data, observations of teaching, and interactions with colleagues to report student achievement and opportunities to learn to students, teachers, parents, policy makers, and the general public.

Continues on next page

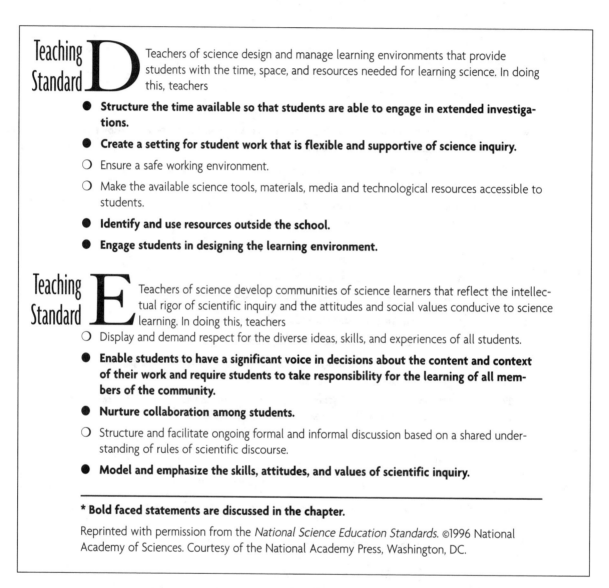

Teaching Standard D Teachers of science design and manage learning environments that provide students with the time, space, and resources needed for learning science. In doing this, teachers

- **Structure the time available so that students are able to engage in extended investigations.**
- **Create a setting for student work that is flexible and supportive of science inquiry.**
- ○ Ensure a safe working environment.
- ○ Make the available science tools, materials, media and technological resources accessible to students.
- **Identify and use resources outside the school.**
- **Engage students in designing the learning environment.**

Teaching Standard E Teachers of science develop communities of science learners that reflect the intellectual rigor of scientific inquiry and the attitudes and social values conducive to science learning. In doing this, teachers

- ○ Display and demand respect for the diverse ideas, skills, and experiences of all students.
- **Enable students to have a significant voice in decisions about the content and context of their work and require students to take responsibility for the learning of all members of the community.**
- **Nurture collaboration among students.**
- ○ Structure and facilitate ongoing formal and informal discussion based on a shared understanding of rules of scientific discourse.
- **Model and emphasize the skills, attitudes, and values of scientific inquiry.**

---

* Bold faced statements are discussed in the chapter.

Reprinted with permission from the *National Science Education Standards*. ©1996 National Academy of Sciences. Courtesy of the National Academy Press, Washington, DC.

Adapting Labs
and Troubleshooting

A great deal of information is available on how children learn—brain research, multiple intelligence aspects, concrete versus abstract thinking, environmental stimuli, and so on—but one key feature can be gleaned from all of the studies, and that is the importance of hands-on learning (see Resources). No matter what method students use to garner information, the learning process can be augmented with the inclusion of labs, activities, or simulations that mimic real-life experiences. This is especially true in the middle school science classroom. According to the National Science Teachers Association (NSTA 1990), 80 percent of middle school classroom science instruction needs to involve hands-on experiences, so let's get to it.

Initially, you should turn to your science textbook and resource package for lab activities that have been prepared by the textbook authors to follow the information and concepts in the student textbook. These activities can be used to introduce a unit of study, explore a particular concept or idea, investigate a scientific fact or law, or experiment with apparatus or models. Many times the labs are completely written with background information, impetus, instructions, data tables, illustrations, charts, and questions all ready for the copy machine. Some labs, however, may require materials you do not have or cannot purchase due to budget constraints. Or perhaps the lab premise is good, but the activity seems lacking in some respect. This is

when you need to do outside searching, adapting, and writing of labs.

Looking for Labs

Many, many resource books are available for science teachers—like the one you have opened to this page. If you can focus on a specific area of science—such as Earth science—or unit of study—simple machines—that will help narrow the field of sources. There are websites galore, full of lesson plans with labs geared toward practically any science subject. Use other website links and bibliographic information in the search. Check out the school library, corporation or school professional library, local library or university library for titles of interest—books or magazines that emphasize science or education, or both. Ask the teachers at your school or in your school district for any resource materials or leads they may have to share. Bookstores generally have an education section and a children's section that may have books on science experiments. Check out the books in "NSTA Recommends" on the NSTA website.

As mentioned in Chapter 3, science kits can conveniently meet middle school lab and activity needs. Many science supply and textbook catalogs have inquiry-based series or science kits to choose from and include a section of ancillary materials, some of which can be previewed for a period of time—usually 30 days—before you decide to buy.

SCILINKS.
THE WORLD'S A CLICK AWAY

Topic: using models
Go to: www.scilinks.org
Code: HMS47

Inspect the exhibits at science conventions or education conferences. Many textbook and science resource companies have sample books, kits, or other materials available. The science departments at your local universities and colleges may be able to provide resources and tips.

Adapting Labs

Do not overlook the resources aimed at elementary or high school grades. Why? Read on. A middle school science teacher can take any lab and adapt it for classroom purposes and lesson objectives. It is a matter of gearing up or watering down terminology that sounds instructionally inferior but is educationally sound. Activities meant for elementary age students can be geared up with some subtle changes, and activities targeted to adults or older students can be watered down for middle school students to do on their own.

To adapt activities aimed at younger students, you can

- Add questions that require higher order thinking skills—skills that enhance your students' abilities to analyze, separate, order, connect, arrange, divide, select, infer, plan, create, design, invent, ask what if, compose, formulate, generalize, rewrite, assess, rank, grade, test, recommend, convince, select, judge, support, conclude, and summarize
- Require charts, tables, and graphs to be created from collected data
- Include the activity in a group of related labs (called stations or rotational lab)
- Let the activity function as a student-written formal lab report using the various scientific method steps including identifying controls and variables
- Treat the activity as an introduction to a concept or unit that will build from its simple premise.

Lab experiences more attuned to high school students can be diluted in a number of ways. You can

- Demonstrate an activity yourself if it calls for chemicals or material that are too hazardous for middle school students. It is important to follow the procedures listed in Chapter 4 to ensure safety or try to find safer substitutes.
- Use chunking, breaking down and rewriting detailed questions or instructions into simpler chunks
- Simplify table and graph directions
- Arrange larger cooperative student lab groups and divide the lab work among them (See Chapter 10, Scenario Two, for ideas)
- Supply formulas, tips, or hints for math calculations
- Use vocabulary words as pre-lab definition words or ask the English teacher to use the words as spelling or vocabulary words (interdisciplinary!)
- Convert a one-day high school lab into a two- or three-day middle school lab.

Reinforcing Inquiry

After finding labs and making them middle-school friendly, you may wish to make these hands-on experiences more inquiry based. The importance of hands-on science and the various types of inquiry instruction were outlined in Chapter 3. Here are some ideas you can use to implement this type of investigation. Start inquiry by introducing the activity in a way that prompts student questioning and discussing. You can

- Create an opening scenario or situation. If the purpose of the lesson is to provide a tangible experience relating the physics and mathematics of energy, friction, momentum, and gravity, a situation like this could be used: "You are on a team of builders working on a new roller coaster for a theme park. The owners of the theme park would like this new ride to include some curves and loops as well as inclines and straight tracks to provide ample thrills to people riding in the

roller coaster cars. Your team must design and build a working model, then give a presentation to the board of directors demonstrating your model on (date)." This prompts students to begin thinking, discussing, and questioning.

- Present a demonstration activity to the class in a way that produces student discussion and questioning. For example, you can use a paper rocket simulation for student observation and discussion leading to Newton's third law of motion and rocket propulsion, basic rocket design, and flight duration and direction (Farenga, Joyce, and Dowling 2002).

- Lay out some materials on desks or a common area in the classroom. Curiosity will force some students to pick the items up, look at them, try them out, show others in class, and finally ask the teacher, "What are we doing today?" or "Are we going to work with these things today?" or perhaps even "What are these things for?" Then prompt them to suggest answers themselves and develop more questions.

Another way to adapt labs for inquiry is to ask questions about the procedures or instructions. While students are occupied with the lab activity, pose open-ended or divergent questions to stimulate student inquiry: "Tell me about your ..." "What does this mean to you?" "What could you do instead?" "How are you going to do that?" "Is there anything else you could use?" and so on. Wait a few seconds for student responses, and avoid giving any advice or criticism verbally or through gestures or expressions.

After the investigation has ended and assessment is completed, you can offer students opportunities to share products with others, allow them to complete extension activities that might involve further research and design, and help students still at a low level of understanding with some direct instruction from you or from peers (Colburn 2000).

Modifying for Special Needs Students

The modifying job may not yet be over. In many middle school classrooms, teachers have special education or ESL students along with very highly able students in their classroom mix. These students require some altered versions of labs, too. You can make adjustments by using the simpler elementary questions along with one or two higher order thinking skills for the lower-ability students and leaving some of the high school terminology in the directions and questions for students needing to be challenged. You can also turn to the special needs and ESL teachers for assistance and guidance, great resources any time modifications are made.

Troubleshooting Labs

Troubleshooting in the lab is not as technical as it may sound; in fact, it can be very simple. First, and foremost, always perform the lab yourself before you ask students to do it. This may be a "duh" factor to you, but there are teachers who download labs, make copies, and believe they are ready for the next day. You need to check that instructions are clear and organized, to check that there are enough lab materials and to examine their condition, to calculate the time needed — resources usually give a time allotment, but always verify it—and to anticipate any questions students may have. Even if you've done the lab in the past, repeat it to renew your memory. A first-time classroom lab, even if you have tried it, can bring changes. Keep a copy of the lab handy to make notations for improvement the next time.

To maintain all equipment in good working order,
- Clean Bunsen burners with pipe cleaners— a little acid bath may be in order to remove corrosion, make sure burner hoses are clear, and check gas nozzles and handles
- Inspect glassware for chips or breaks

- Ensure equipment is plugged in, and check for frayed cords or plugs
- Verify whether or not emergency stops are turned off
- Reset electrical outlets
- Ensure bulbs work
- Ensure plenty of soap and paper towels are available in the dispensers at lab areas
- Invest in some common household tools: screwdrivers of various sizes, hammers, wire cutters, needle nose pliers, and regular pliers.

Experience, of course, will increase your troubleshooting skills as the years pass, but sometimes we tend to overlook the simplest problems, especially in this increasingly technological society.

When you find an activity that fills the bill and make the necessary adaptations, keep it on file, although you may need to make revisions and modifications throughout the time the activities are used. Troubleshooting skills and experience will help guarantee your students' hands-on experiences go smoothly. Before long, you'll become the expert others will turn to.

References

Farenga, S. J., B. A. Joyce, and T. W. Dowling. 2002. Rocketing into adaptive inquiry. *Science Scope* 25 (4): 34–39.

Colburn, A. 2000. An inquiry primer. *Science Scope* 23 (6): 42–44.

National Science Teachers Association (NSTA) Board of Directors. Adopted in January 1990. *NSTA Position Statement*. NSTA Committees and Task Forces. Retrieved January 29, 2002, from *www.nsta.org/159&id=16*

Resources

Book/Print Sources

Sarquis, M., and J. Sarquis. 1991. *Fun with chemistry*. Madison, WI: Institute for Chemical Education (ICE Publication 91-005). (labs and activities plus an appendix with a list of chemicals, common names, and where these can be purchased)

Web Source URLs

Please note that websites are often changed, deleted and moved.

Website	Subject
How children learn	
www.sedl.org/scimath/compass/v03n02/1.html	best practices in science education
www.angelfire.com/oh/themidas/index.html	best practices in science education
www.ldrc.ca/projects/miinventory/miinventory.php?eightstyles=1	best practices in science education
www.ed.gov/databases/ERIC_Digests/ed410226.html	best practices in science education
www.cudenver.edu/~mryder/itc_data/constructivism.html	best practices in science education
www.mcgill.ca/douglas/fdg/kjf/17-TAGLA.htm.	best practices in science education
tip.psychology.org/bruner.html	best practices in science education
www.mcps.k12.md.us/departments/eventscience/Origins.html	best practices in science education
www.hardin.k12.ky.us/res_techn/grrec/webquest/science_best_practices.htm	best practices in science education

www.mcps.k12.md.us/departments/eii/bestpracticespg.htm .... best practices in science education

mdk12.org/practices/good_instruction/projectbetter/
science/index.html .... best practices in science education

www.exploratorium.edu/IFI/ .... best practices in science education

Lesson plan sites

www.chem4kids.com/

www.biology4kids.com/

www.geography4kids.com/ .... ecology/environment

www.physics4kids.com/

school.discovery.com/lessonplans/index.html

www.opticalres.com/kidoptx.html

www.brainpop.com/

www.physicalscienceseries.com/programs.htm

scifun.chem.wisc.edu/

www.energyquest.ca.gov/index.html

Demonstrations

www.sciencenetlinks.com/matrix.cfm .... teacher demonstrations for safety

scied.unl.edu/pages/mamres/pages/demos/demo.html .... science demonstrations

scied.unl.edu/pages/mamres/pages/demos/physical/physical.htm .. science demonstrations

scied.unl.edu/pages/sciencedemos/index.htm .... science demonstrations

www.itg.lbl.gov/ITG.hm.pg.docs/dissect/info.html .... virtual frog dissection

www.epa.gov/region7/education_resources/teachers/
ehsstudy/ehs12.htm .... suggestions and additional sites for chemical
alternatives

www.thecatalyst.org/hwrp/safetymanual/earth_space_concerns.html

Science kit retailers other than school science catalogs

www.einsteins-emporium.com/

www.discoverthis.com/

www.terrifictoy.com/

www.thinkertoyscarmel.com/

www.pishtoys.com/index.html

National Science Education Standards Note:

*This chapter specifically addresses Teaching Standard A, bullet points two, three, and four; and Teaching Standard D, bullet points one, two, and five.

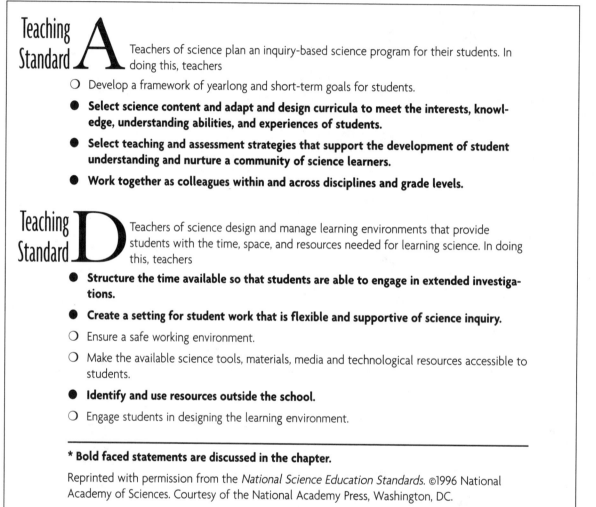

Teaching Standard A Teachers of science plan an inquiry-based science program for their students. In doing this, teachers

○ Develop a framework of yearlong and short-term goals for students.

● **Select science content and adapt and design curricula to meet the interests, knowledge, understanding abilities, and experiences of students.**

● **Select teaching and assessment strategies that support the development of student understanding and nurture a community of science learners.**

● **Work together as colleagues within and across disciplines and grade levels.**

Teaching Standard D Teachers of science design and manage learning environments that provide students with the time, space, and resources needed for learning science. In doing this, teachers

● **Structure the time available so that students are able to engage in extended investigations.**

● **Create a setting for student work that is flexible and supportive of science inquiry.**

○ Ensure a safe working environment.

○ Make the available science tools, materials, media and technological resources accessible to students.

● **Identify and use resources outside the school.**

○ Engage students in designing the learning environment.

***

* Bold faced statements are discussed in the chapter.

Reprinted with permission from the *National Science Education Standards.* ©1996 National Academy of Sciences. Courtesy of the National Academy Press, Washington, DC.

Modeling and Demonstrations

ELLEN JOY SASAKI

You could smell the excitement in the air, or perhaps it was just the preservation fluid. It was frog dissection day in the seventh grade.

   As students entered the room, Mr. Kemper directed their attention to the TV screen. They watched in awe as he unveiled a dissection tray, complete with frog, and placed it under the visual presenter (aka Elmo) that projected onto the TV screen.

   Kemper explained that he would demonstrate the beginning steps of dissection on the screen, and then the students would move to their own lab stations to dissect their own specimen.

As he showed how to pin the frog and carefully open its abdomen without destroying the underlying organs, he could see relief flood the faces of the most apprehensive students. They felt better having seen that what lay beneath a frog's skin would not make them vomit. As well, he could see the excitement build on the faces of those who had been asking for months, "When do we get to dissect?"

Once the demonstration was over, the students began working on their own frogs, carefully following Kemper's lead. For many, this was their first experience with scalpel and scissors, and the few minutes of watching before beginning made all the difference.

One common misconception in the middle school science classroom is that students magically will know how to do many of the seemingly easy tasks teachers assign. In reality, even the simple direction of using written resources to gain background information can cause consternation for students and teachers. To alleviate this problem you can use the easy, yet effective, method of modeling classroom activities (see Chapter 3, "Best Practices").

Modeling can reduce the number of times students ask for clarification. It can establish appropriate and scientifically sound classroom techniques for future use, and it can produce results that meet the requirements set by you and your school district's science curriculum. Here are some typical science class activities and how modeling can be used in each instance.

Using Written Resources

After pointing out the text to be read, you should model the appropriate reading practices by reading aloud a page or two from the assignment. Prior to beginning reading, note some important aspects of the written resource that will help the students with unfamiliar terms or concepts, such as the location of the glossary, index, or appendices. It is also important to note for the students various ancillary items in the text that may aid their understanding and to tell them how they should use those items:

- Titles and section headings denote the specific subject or concept being studied and can help students locate specific sections when working on assignments or preparing for tests.
- Bold or italicized print terms sometimes are used to highlight words important to the subject's or concept's meaning and can help students when working on vocabulary development.
- Captions and pictures can help students grasp difficult topics by providing additional references.
- Diagrams, charts, and/or graphs explain mathematical aspects of the concept and can show difficult numerical explanations in a visual format.

SCiLINKS.
THE WORLD'S A CLICK AWAY
Topic: developing
classroom activities
Go to: www.scilinks.org
Code: HMS54

- Summaries recap what students have read and can help them prepare for tests or assigned projects.

Next, begin reading the text aloud and refer to the ancillary items verbally. Be very descriptive, include everything, even "reading" a graph or wondering aloud what the boldface vocabulary term might mean, then referring to the glossary or index for additional information. You can model being confused about a text reference or term and writing down that reference or term and the page number to ask for clarification later. Be sure to point out that reading further in the text can provide clarification. Even though students may giggle at your exaggerated reading process, you will make your point, and your students will be more likely to read for understanding when they begin the process themselves. Although this is an appropriate modeling demonstration for the beginning of the year, it is important to revisit the process often so students will not fall out of their good reading habits.

The Writing Process

Any writing task should include the following information when you make the assignment:

Type of writing—lab report, commentary, summary, essay, evaluation

Content—information gleaned from the text or other reference, compare/contrast concepts, cause/effect explanations, persuasive writing, topical or historical writing

Assessment using a sample rubric—posted in the room in a highly visible area, individual copies handed out to each student when assigned, or explained through class discussion via an overhead transparency

Many schools have prescribed standards for writing based on state and national standards. It is important to remind students that the standards for writing in the science classroom are the same as those in the language arts classroom. (See the next section for hints on working with the language arts department.) Model the writing process by writing on chalkboard, chart paper, or butcher paper, or using an overhead so students can see a well-written example to use as a guide for their writing. Again, think aloud while working through the assignment. You can use outlines, jot lists, paragraph planners, or other templates as a starting point. Using the formats from the language arts department will help build continuity between the disciplines. As you demonstrate writing the rough draft, use students as proofreaders, helping check for spelling, grammar, and sentence structure. If a sentence or passage sounds awkward, ask for suggestions. Make sure you have a dictionary and thesaurus handy. When the writing task is completed, compare it to the rubric and go through the checklist aloud, making changes as necessary. Students will see the purpose of a rough draft and the need for a final copy. (Return to Chapter 6 for information on writing.)

Help from the Language Arts Department

When you assign written tasks, you will find consulting your school's language arts department helpful for numerous reasons. Language arts teachers

- Can use your assignment as a "mini-interdisciplinary" lesson in their own classes. This helps show your students how interconnected subjects are and gives them ample time to proofread and edit their work.
- Can help your students organize their pre-writing, edit their rough drafts, and produce a finished piece of work by providing samples of graphic organizers
- Can help with spelling and grammar troubles and teach appropriate methods for writing that

are common to science, such as comparing and contrasting and persuasive essays.

If your school has a spelling program, many language arts teachers are willing to include key vocabulary terms from science class in their spelling lessons to help reinforce those terms.

Take some time at the beginning of each unit of study to talk with your language arts department and let them know what you are planning. You will find an invaluable resource that will not only make your job easier but also provide your students with enriched lessons in science and language arts.

Experimenting in Lab

Before you start, remember that safety and proper apparatus use are extremely important in the science lab. If students are required to wear goggles and apron, the teacher needs to wear them, too. The reverse is true when the teacher is doing a classroom lab demonstration; if the teacher is wearing safety apparel, so should the students. It takes only one accident to have a lifetime of regret. (For more information on lab set-up and safety, see Chapter 4.)

Demonstration is a tried and true modeling process for the science classroom. Take the time to show students how to light a Bunsen burner, and the striker flints will be longer-lived. Show the entire class how to use a graduated cylinder and a small rock to calculate the volume of an irregular solid, and you will not become frustrated showing the process repeatedly to small lab groups. Demonstrate how to use the ruler when measuring length or distance, and students will know which side is the metric side.

One of the biggest difficulties with lab demonstrations is making sure everyone can see what is going on. You may need to repeat the demonstration, breaking the class into smaller groups and making sure the others are occupied with another task, or use special equipment, such as a videotape of the demonstration, overhead mirror (found in science catalogs), a visual camera presenter with a live video camera feed, or a computer microscope.

As with the reading and writing modeling, verbalize all the steps and thought processes while you are doing the demonstration. Not only can you exhibit good safety habits and lab practices, but you can also include troubleshooting techniques for common lab problems. For example, if the microscope image is fuzzy, verbalize the steps in your fine-tuning techniques. If the burner flame needs adjusting, think aloud as you make alterations.

Sometimes demonstrations are preferred to small group lab activity because lab supplies are insufficient or safety issues go beyond the normal lab routines. You may prefer demonstrating to the entire class how zinc and hydrochloric acid can produce hydrogen gas, then using a lit splint to identify that gas rather than risking a Hindenburg-like explosion. When you are verbalizing results and safety instructions, you are limiting the safety concerns.

Information Research Techniques

This topic fits into the writing instruction session, but it deserves its own explanation here because of its importance to the study of scientific concepts. Again, the teacher should check the school standards for writing based on state and national standards and review any of the requirements —note cards, works-cited page, footnoting, and parenthetical citation—before starting the research process. If any students are unsure of any requirement, either the teacher or another pupil can model the procedure for them. As we said, think aloud through the process: choosing a topic, coming up with related topics or keywords, and deciding where to look for resources —newspapers, periodicals, books, and websites. Show stu-

dents how to search on the computer, either in a classroom setup or in a computer lab, before letting them turn on their own computers. Use library media retrieval —electronic card catalog, card catalog, *Readers' Guide to Periodical Literature*, and CD-ROMs—then think aloud as periodicals are found, encyclopedias are thumbed through, and brief citations are written down. Orally instruct students in the best practices of searching the different sources: referring to the indexes of reference books, skimming the table of contents or preface of a book, reading the first paragraph and last as well as the first sentence of the paragraphs in between of a magazine or newspaper article, and using any reading and writing techniques previously modeled.

Another approach to searching for information is to create a scavenger hunt that could be used as a contest or incentive activity. Scavenger hunts are a great way for a teacher to guide students' learning of the processes of research, for students to acquire background information prior to the study of a particular concepts, and for students to form an educated prediction (hypothesis) when beginning a lab experiment. Contact the media specialist in your school for help in developing the scavenger hunt. Or you can create an electronic quest using Internet sources, and CD-ROMs of encyclopedias and other reference books; look online for a research Web quest; or make up your own Web quest. Some students might be interested in creating their own library scavenger hunts or Web quests. This involves some time initially, but once the template is made, updating it in succeeding years will go quickly. And remember that a rubric can be a checklist for students to use as well as a guide to clear expectations for assessment.

Modeling is an important part of providing instruction and building essential skills, particularly in the science classroom. Although students come to us with a variety of experiences and abilities, modeling can bring all of them up to speed on science skills, making it a most useful device in any teacher's bag of tricks.

National Science Education Standards Note:

*This chapter specifically addresses Teaching Standard A, bullet point two; and Teaching Standard B, bullet point five.

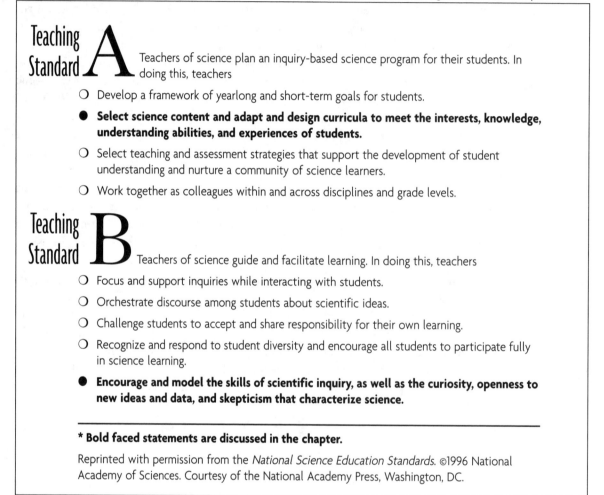

Teaching
Standard A Teachers of science plan an inquiry-based science program for their students. In doing this, teachers

○ Develop a framework of yearlong and short-term goals for students.

● **Select science content and adapt and design curricula to meet the interests, knowledge, understanding abilities, and experiences of students.**

○ Select teaching and assessment strategies that support the development of student understanding and nurture a community of science learners.

○ Work together as colleagues within and across disciplines and grade levels.

Teaching
Standard B Teachers of science guide and facilitate learning. In doing this, teachers

○ Focus and support inquiries while interacting with students.

○ Orchestrate discourse among students about scientific ideas.

○ Challenge students to accept and share responsibility for their own learning.

○ Recognize and respond to student diversity and encourage all students to participate fully in science learning.

● **Encourage and model the skills of scientific inquiry, as well as the curiosity, openness to new ideas and data, and skepticism that characterize science.**

---

* Bold faced statements are discussed in the chapter.

Reprinted with permission from the *National Science Education Standards*. ©1996 National Academy of Sciences. Courtesy of the National Academy Press, Washington, DC.

Metrics and Measurement

One of the most challenging activities in the middle school science lab is taking measurements. A simple ruler can send students into a questioning mob around a teacher, not unlike a shark-feeding frenzy. Student activities that require using and reading a thermometer can cause teachers to lose their hair from the strain of pulling on it with frustration. Then there is the dread of teaching metrics, or the SI system (International System of Units) as it is now termed in most science texts. However, these training exercises can have the opposite effect when designed for practice and application.

As a start, you may want to review briefly the history of measurement or brainstorm with the class why measurement is important.

Why Have a Standard System?

To duplicate experiments or share information, the science community needs a language of measurement that is uniform and easy to use and understand. Scientists worldwide use the SI. It is based on units of 10, just like the number system students already understand, and is easy to manipulate by dividing or multiplying by 10. Your students will understand the need to have the same system of measurement, but they may argue that SI is not as easy to use or understand as the familiar English system. To show this may not be true, a teacher can quiz students about this "familiar" system by asking questions such as how many bushels are in a peck, drams in an ounce, or furlongs in a mile. (See Appendix A, p. 99, for examples). These questions are difficult for the average student, and many may not have heard of a dram or furlong. The questions may spur interest in metrics, making students willing to learn the easier SI measurements.

The Stair-Step Method

A most useful tool for introducing metric prefixes and easy conversion from one prefix to the next is the stair-step method. This method uses the simple premise of changes that are made by moving up and down a staircase as in Figure 9.1, next page. One of the steps is noted as the unit. The steps above and below the unit step correspond to the different metric prefixes, symbols, and their numeric values, increasing in value as the steps go up and decreasing as the steps go down. (See Appendix A, p. 101, for a copy.)

You can use an actual staircase if there is one at school or copy Figure 9.1 onto chart paper, chalkboard, or wipe board to demonstrate its use while students refer to their own copies. First point out the shaded box and read the statement inside. The three most frequently used measures in SI are meter (m), liter (L), and gram (g). Make sure to use these symbols as well as those of the prefixes when demonstrating the stair-step method. Point out that prefixes are not words when they stand alone; they must have a root word following. So, depending on the measurement being taken, a unit is coupled with the prefix, like centigram or cg. If the measured unit has only one "m," it **always** stands for meter, not milli.

SC**I**LINKS.
THE WORLD'S A CLICK AWAY

Topic: metric system
Go to: www.scilinks.org
Code: HMS59

Figure 9.1

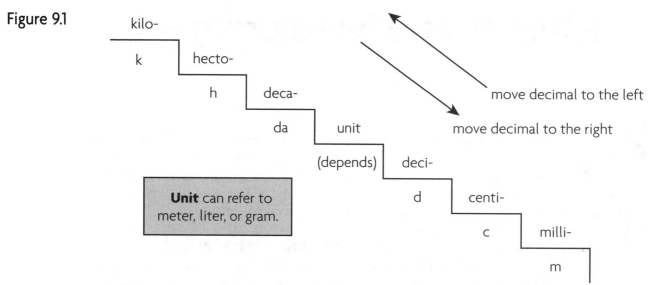

move decimal to the left

move decimal to the right

kilo-
k

hecto-
h

deca-
da

unit
(depends)

deci-
d

centi-
c

milli-
m

Unit can refer to meter, liter, or gram.

Begin by writing a sample conversion problem such as 23.675 cg = _____ hg. Point out that the "g" in cg stands for grams and the "c" is for the prefix "centi." Then explain that the "g" in hg again stands for grams while the "h" is for the prefix "hecto." On the stairstep, start at the step labeled centi- (**X**) in Figure 9.2 and count the number of steps up to the step labeled hecto-. Because it took four steps to get to hecto- and the direction of the move was **up** the stairs, the decimal point in the problem will be moved four steps to the left. Therefore 23.675 cg = .0023675 hg. Students can readily see that moving up the stairs involves dividing by 10 (moving the decimal point to the left), while moving down the stairs entails multiplying by 10 (moving the decimal point to

Figure 9.2

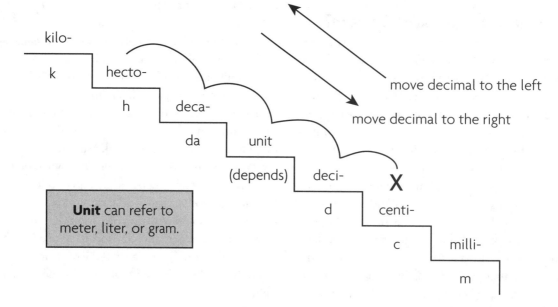

move decimal to the left

move decimal to the right

kilo-
k

hecto-
h

deca-
da

unit
(depends)

deci-
d

X

centi-
c

milli-
m

Unit can refer to meter, liter, or gram.

the right). Again, practice is important to learn symbols, prefixes, units, and conversion (See Appendix A, p. 102, for worksheet).

Practice Makes Perfect

Middle school students have had measurement activities in the past, but take the time to refresh memories. Have measurement instruments out for students to view or even touch—they could even be questioned as to how they think the device is used or what it can measure. Some possible instruments to show them are balances; scales; graduated containers like cylinders, flasks, or beakers; stopwatches; standard and metric rulers; yardsticks; meter sticks; and thermometers. You can model using the instruments while thinking aloud and even asking for student help. Point out the "parts" of the instrument, the marks (½, ¼, ¾, etc.) on a standard ruler; the marks (cm and mm) on a metric ruler; how to use and read a stopwatch; the art of reading a measure on a graduated cylinder using the meniscus, or using a balance depending on type—for example, electronic, triple beam, scale with weights.

You may want to show your students the graduation on the containers, balances, and thermometers to determine the number interval being used and how to "read" the marks (see Appendix A, p. 103, for a sample worksheet). Practice makes perfect holds true with measuring devices. Students can practice using each instrument after you have modeled it or manipulate the devices in stations you have set up (see Appendix A, p. 104, for a sample station lab).

Students need to recognize that the SI and English systems can be compared and that changing from one system to another is possible. For example, students are very familiar with the Fahrenheit scale and may also have heard temperatures given in

Celsius, but they probably have no experience with the Kelvin scale. Since these are all used for the same quantitative measure, their scales can be changed from one to the other using mathematical formulas. Some science textbooks list these conversions, or equivalencies can be found in some reference books like an almanac, encyclopedia, or in this book (see Appendix A, p. 106).

Everyday Use

Knowing how to use these conversions can have some practical applications, as illustrated in the following project. Tell students to bring in a recipe for some type of homemade cookies and challenge them to change the ingredient amounts to metric measure. Then they can show conversion formulas used and the calculations made during this cookie exchange. Maybe the family and consumer science—what used to be known as home economics—teacher and the math teacher would like to get in on this activity, too. Another way of looking at measurement standards is to make up units using familiar words, phrases, or puns (see Appendix A, p. 107).

Measurements in the science lab are definitely necessary components of sharing data and comparing results. Students should use measurement techniques, instruments, and conversion methods as often as they can in a variety of activities to become comfortable with SI. About 25 years ago, the push was for the United States to go "metric" to make our everyday system of measurement match the one used by virtually the rest of the world. This led to bottling liquids in 1- and 2-liter containers, but little else. If today's students learn SI measurement and become comfortable using and applying this system, then, as consumers of tomorrow, they may not hesitate to adopt the metric approach.

National Science Education Standards Note:

*This chapter specifically addresses Teaching Standard A, bullet point three, and Teaching Standard B, bullet point five.

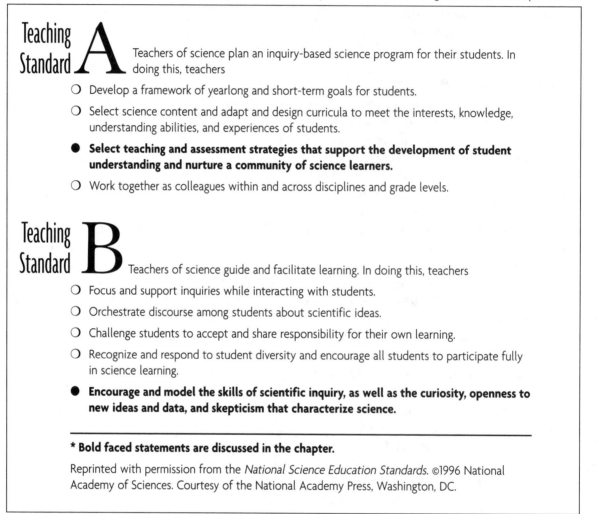

Teaching
Standard A

Teachers of science plan an inquiry-based science program for their students. In doing this, teachers

○ Develop a framework of yearlong and short-term goals for students.

○ Select science content and adapt and design curricula to meet the interests, knowledge, understanding abilities, and experiences of students.

● **Select teaching and assessment strategies that support the development of student understanding and nurture a community of science learners.**

○ Work together as colleagues within and across disciplines and grade levels.

Teaching
Standard B

Teachers of science guide and facilitate learning. In doing this, teachers

○ Focus and support inquiries while interacting with students.

○ Orchestrate discourse among students about scientific ideas.

○ Challenge students to accept and share responsibility for their own learning.

○ Recognize and respond to student diversity and encourage all students to participate fully in science learning.

● **Encourage and model the skills of scientific inquiry, as well as the curiosity, openness to new ideas and data, and skepticism that characterize science.**

---

* Bold faced statements are discussed in the chapter.

Reprinted with permission from the *National Science Education Standards*. ©1996 National Academy of Sciences. Courtesy of the National Academy Press, Washington, DC.

Classroom Management

ELLEN JOY SASAKI

Perhaps the most important skill a good teacher should possess is the ability to control students. A teacher who can devise fascinating and unique lesson plans for her classroom is useless if she can't get the kids to sit down and listen to her instructions.

Useless? Pretty harsh words, you say?

Unfortunately, many beginning teachers simply are not prepared to manage their classrooms effectively. Managing a classroom means you must teach your students behavior expectations, not just post your rules on the classroom wall. Classroom management becomes even more of an issue when it applies to the active nature of the science classroom. The negative results of ineffective classroom management strategies are twofold:

- The students fail to learn basic concepts because the distractions of an uncontrolled classroom make it impossible to concentrate fully on the subject at hand.

- The teacher, in an effort to regain control, often abandons proven best practices, such as hands-on activities and cooperative learning, for "traditional" techniques that keep the students at their desks and at their textbooks for the duration of the class period.

Even if you feel your teaching strengths do not lie in the management category, there is hope. Implementing some proven and simple classroom management strategies can help you avoid uncontrolled situations. Three typical scenarios are outlined below, shown first as ineffectively managed and then effectively managed.

Scenario One: The Beginning of Class

The Ineffective Classroom—*Students are congregating in various locations around the room, chatting about the latest gossip. Several girls have their mirrors and lipsticks out. A handful of boys are trying to leap high enough to touch the doorjamb or push the ceiling tiles out of their frames. The shy students sit in their seats nervously watching the other students, wondering why they are the only ones who don't have a lot of friends talking to them.*

Mr. Chen is frantically trying to find make-up work for a student who has been absent while trying to settle the class down with verbal warnings. The principal walks in and asks to speak to Chen in the hallway about an afternoon committee meeting. When the bell rings, students race around the room and over the desks to make it to their seats before it stops. As Chen re-enters, the room, the chatting and restlessness continue. He spends the next two or three minutes asking the students to quiet down and reminding them of the tardy policy. Finally, he begins his lesson plan feeling rushed and frustrated.

The Effective Classroom—*Students arrive in the classroom and find the overhead projector turned on with a message from Mr. Chen on the screen.*

SC*I*LINKS.
THE WORLD'S A CLICK AWAY

Topic: classroom
management
Go to: *www.scilinks.org*
Code: HMS64

Figure 10.1

> Today is Tuesday, March 10th. I'm glad you are here today!
> Please be sure to do the following <u>before</u> the bell rings:
> 1. Say hello to the person who sits to your left.
> 2. Copy down today's homework assignment in your daily planner.
> 3. Get out a sheet of paper and head it properly for today's lab.
> 4. Read the lab introduction you find on page 33 in your lab notebook.

The students say their hellos and sit down in their seats to begin copying the homework assignment. A shy student smiles slightly because the most popular kid in the class has just said "hello" to him. Chen is explaining missed work to a student who has been absent. The bell rings, and the students become quiet as they begin reading their lab introduction. Chen gently asks a student who is talking to her neighbor, "Amy, have you completed everything on the overhead?" Amy sheepishly shakes her head and then quickly gets to work. The principal walks in and tells Chen about how "good his kids are." Chen and the principal briefly discuss the afternoon's committee meeting and then class begins.

Any educational expert will tell you the first few minutes of class determine the tone and success of the remainder of the class. (Wong and Wong 1998) Thus, it is important you plan the first few minutes to help students focus on science class and not on what happened at lunch or out in the hallway. Planning the first few minutes—which don't have to relate directly to the day's lesson—is not difficult. The purpose is to get the students in the room and focused on learning. These guidelines will help get your classes off to a great start.

Plan activities the students can do without your assistance. You will always have responsibilities at the beginning of the period that require your full attention—hallway duty, taking roll, assisting special needs students, bringing students who have been absent up to speed on missed work. Your students need to be able to get started without direct supervision. This not only gives you a chance to complete other duties but also teaches the students the valuable skill of self-discipline.

Use an overhead projector or the chalkboard to explain clearly what you want the students doing when they walk in the room. Convey your instructions in a positive tone, but be very straightforward so even your lower-level students can understand what you expect.

Have a variety of activities for students to do during the first few minutes of class. Examples of activities include reading a paragraph from the text that applies to the day's lesson, writing a journal entry about a topic you give them, working out a word problem or riddle, copying a quote from a famous scientist into their daily planners, writing down two things they learned from the previous day's lesson, and more. The possibilities are endless, and, as long it gets the students focused on learning, it works.

Don't limit yourself to only science-related activities. We all know our students can use practice in their other subjects as well. Feel free to put a math word problem or a sentence that needs to be corrected on the board. Your colleagues will appreciate your willingness to integrate their subjects into your classroom, and you will still have accomplished your goal of focusing your students on learning when they walk through your classroom door.

Scenario Two: Group Projects and Group Labs

The Ineffective Classroom—*From the hallway, you can hear Mrs. Carter shouting out the same instructions for the day's project over and over. That's because she is surrounded by groups of students asking the same question over and over. Students are wandering around the room, looking for supplies, and asking each other, "Now what are we supposed to be doing again?" A group in the back of the room has lost interest in the project and is looking out the window at the gym class outside on the basketball courts. Carter tries to settle the students down, but they are all so lost no one seems to be listening. She looks at her watch and realizes, at this rate, they will never get the project done before the end of the period. She sighs with frustration and wonders why she didn't just assign the questions at the end of the chapter instead of working hard on planning a project.*

The Effective Classroom—*Before the students are released from their seats to begin working in groups, Mrs. Carter reads the instructions for that day's project aloud and points out where the supplies students will need are located. She asks the students if they have any questions. After answering the questions that have been asked, she instructs the group to assign the following job titles and responsibilities to a member of each group.*

- *Group Timekeeper. This person is in charge of making sure everyone is on task and working and also keeps the group informed of how much time they have left.*
- *Group Inquiry Representative. This person takes any questions the group has to the teacher for answers.*
- *Group Recorder. This person is in charge of making sure all written or produced work gets done and given to the teacher at the proper time and place.*
- *Group Supplies Manager. This person is in charge of collecting necessary supplies when the group gets started. Supplies managers also make sure the area their groups work in and the supplies they use are cleaned up and in their proper storage place before they leave the classroom at the end of the period. Once the groups have decided who will do each job, they move to where they can work comfortably and without disturbing other groups. The supplies managers begin picking up supplies while the rest of the groups*

begin discussing the task at hand. Carter moves around the room, giving encouragement and answering questions from the inquiry representatives. As the period draws to a close, the timekeepers encourage their groups to wrap things up. When class is over, the recorders bring the group's work to Carter. She smiles because she knows the students have learned a great deal more using this hands-on, cooperative learning approach than they would had they worked only in the textbook.

Educators almost unanimously agree that hands-on learning and cooperative learning are two of the most effective methods for teaching adolescents. Students' behaviors, however, must be controlled and focused for these learning methods to benefit them. The following guidelines will make group work and labs run smoothly, so your students will gain all the benefits from cooperative learning and hands-on activities:

Have all the supplies needed out and ready before class begins. Make sure the supplies are in an easy-to-access location and you have shown the class what and where everything is before they get started. If you are using lab apparatus, you may need to demonstrate its use as well.

Go over the instructions for the project or the lab before the groups get started. Even though many students can understand written directions without your help, many cannot. Going over directions aloud encourages students to listen and think about what they are doing and may also prompt some initial questions.

Make sure each student has a responsibility in the group. Having one person in charge of each aspect of a project makes the class easier for you to manage. When assigning group jobs, tell students they cannot do the same job they did in the last group project or lab. This ensures all students are responsible for different roles several times during the year and also ensures all students are contributors to the group effort.

Assess the students based on the effort and contribution they made to the group. See Chapter 5 for ways to assess group work.

Scenario Three: Lecture and Note Taking

The Ineffective Classroom— *Ms. Gutierrez announces that today the class will be taking notes about our solar system. She tells the students to take out notebook paper and pencils. She then begins lecturing on the solar system from notes she puts on the overhead projector, explaining the difference between a terrestrial and jovian planet. She asks the class if anyone can name a jovian planet. No one raises a hand. She continues her lecture and changes the overhead to the next topic. Some of the students complain they didn't have time to get notes on the first topic finished. A student who is done copying the notes has*

taken her English homework out and is working on that. Gutierrez, frustrated because her class is not paying attention, scolds the students and tells them that, even though note taking is boring, they have to do it because it is the only way to get a lot of information to them in a short time.

The Effective Classroom—*As class begins, Ms. Gutierrez asks the students if anyone knows whether Earth is a terrestrial or jovian planet. The students guess, and they take a class vote that she writes on the board. She then passes out a three-hole-punched photocopy of her notes with some key words and phrases blanked out. She asks the students to listen as she discusses the solar system they live in and to fill in the notes when they hear or see what goes in the blanks. She puts her notes on the overhead, but uncovers only the portion of the notes she is discussing at that moment. As she comes to the blanks in the notes, she writes in the appropriate answers with a marker so the students can fill in their notes. After they finish the notes for the day, Gutierrez revisits the vote the class took at the beginning of the period. She asks for another vote to see if everyone was listening. She asks for a volunteer to review with the group what the difference between a terrestrial and a jovian planet is and what characteristics of Earth make it terrestrial. At the end of the period, Gutierrez reminds the students to place their three-hole-punched notes into their science binders.*

Note taking is a necessary part of science education because of the large amounts of information students must learn. However, adolescents generally do not have the skills necessary to take good notes without looking at a sample from the teacher. Additionally, long note-taking sessions do not work well with the developmental nature of the young adolescent. Follow these guidelines to make any note taking in your classroom developmentally appropriate:

Blank out key words or phrases on your notes to help keep the students focused. This prevents them from racing ahead of you and then tuning out. It also shows them clearly which parts of the notes are most important to the concept you are teaching.

If your notes are longer than a page, provide students with a three-hole-punched photocopy to use. They can fill in the blanks as you go and underline or highlight other key parts as you discuss the concepts. This procedure may be necessary for special needs students whenever they take notes regardless of the length.

Try to take breaks in the middle of note taking and change activities briefly. Engage the students in a 30 second question-and-answer session about the concepts you just took notes on, then go on to the next section. Have a student volunteer

read from a dictionary the definition of a new vocabulary term you introduced. Have students stand up and briefly act out a topic you have been discussing—for example, water molecules at different temperatures or the revolution of the planets around the sun. A good rule of thumb is to make sure you change activities at least briefly every 10 to 12 minutes to keep the attention of your students. PowerPoint presentations are sometimes more exciting than overhead transparencies—you can add color, graphics, sounds, and videos—and also help break up the monotony of note taking.

Provide three-hole-punched note sheets for the students to use and store in a binder. This also works well for worksheets and tests you may pass back to the students. It is much harder for papers to fall out and get lost.

Use diagrams and graphs in your notes. Young adolescents love to draw and will not even realize they are taking notes and gathering information if they are "just drawing" and labeling diagrams and graphs in their notes.

A Word About Special Needs Students

With state and federal education laws requiring a "least restrictive environment" for students who range from mildly learning disabled to severely and profoundly handicapped, you will most likely have to consider the needs of those students when planning lessons and creating your classroom management plans. These guidelines are extremely important to follow when working with special needs students in your science classroom:

Always consult your school special education teacher when you have questions about a student's ability. Don't ever feel you are bothering a special education teacher if you have a question. They would much rather answer a question before you start than to help you sort out situations that haven't gone well.

Make sure you read each of your special needs students' individualized education plans to know what they are capable of in your classroom. Each student will have a file that will detail things such as reading level, ability to work with others, and the amount of homework he or she is capable of, as well as test-taking procedures and other important topics. The few minutes spent reading a file at the beginning of the year will be worth a great deal of time later as you work with your students.

Be flexible. Be aware from the first day of school that your special needs students have been placed in a special education program for good reason. They have undergone extensive testing by professionals who have determined they need extra help to succeed at school. Special needs students do not learn the same way as other students. At times, you will need to "adjust in flight" to make sure your lesson plans are appropriate for those students. Although you do not want to adjust to the point that your regular education students are not challenged, you need to keep in mind that you may have to individualize your plans for your special needs students on a one-on-one basis.

ESL students can and should learn science. Consult with your English as a Second Language (ESL) specialist to determine the best methods to help your language learners experience as much science as possible while they are acquiring English skills. Copying your notes, providing translated text, or providing extra help with key vocabulary will assist these students and help reduce the boredom and frustration that can lead to misbehavior.

Success Lies Ahead

Classroom management is a skill all successful teachers develop and improve on over the course of their careers. When dealing with difficult students and situations, your veteran colleagues and mentors are a wonderful source of advice and proven methods. Perhaps, though, the best piece of advice we can give you, other than to keep in mind the guidelines in this chapter when planning your lessons, is not to be afraid to try something new and possibly fail. You might just surprise yourself and succeed more than you think.

Reference

Wong, H. K., and R. T. Wong. 1998. *The first days of school: How to be an effective teacher*. Mountain View, CA: Harry K. Wong Publications.

Resources

Book/Print Sources

Center for Early Adolescence. 1985. *Seven developmental needs of young adolescents*. Carrboro, NC: University of North Carolina at Chapel Hill.

Stevenson, C. 1998. *Teaching ten to fourteen year olds*. New York: Longman/Allyn & Bacon. ISBN #0-0813-1582-4 (middle grades teaching textbook)

National Science Education Standards Note:

*This chapter specifically addresses Teaching Standard A, bullet points two and three; Teaching Standard B, bullet point four; Teaching Standard D, bullet point two; and Teaching Standard E, bullet points one and five.

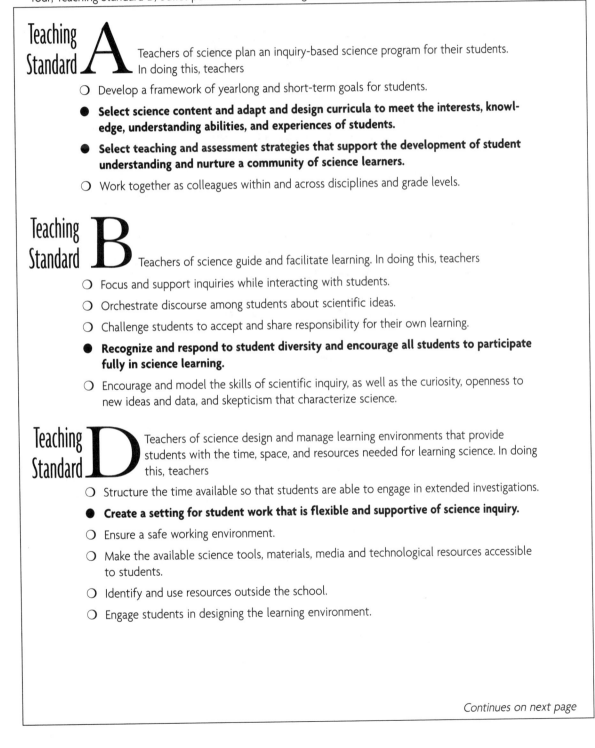

Teaching Standard A

Teachers of science plan an inquiry-based science program for their students. In doing this, teachers

○ Develop a framework of yearlong and short-term goals for students.

● **Select science content and adapt and design curricula to meet the interests, knowledge, understanding abilities, and experiences of students.**

● **Select teaching and assessment strategies that support the development of student understanding and nurture a community of science learners.**

○ Work together as colleagues within and across disciplines and grade levels.

Teaching Standard B

Teachers of science guide and facilitate learning. In doing this, teachers

○ Focus and support inquiries while interacting with students.

○ Orchestrate discourse among students about scientific ideas.

○ Challenge students to accept and share responsibility for their own learning.

● **Recognize and respond to student diversity and encourage all students to participate fully in science learning.**

○ Encourage and model the skills of scientific inquiry, as well as the curiosity, openness to new ideas and data, and skepticism that characterize science.

Teaching Standard D

Teachers of science design and manage learning environments that provide students with the time, space, and resources needed for learning science. In doing this, teachers

○ Structure the time available so that students are able to engage in extended investigations.

● **Create a setting for student work that is flexible and supportive of science inquiry.**

○ Ensure a safe working environment.

○ Make the available science tools, materials, media and technological resources accessible to students.

○ Identify and use resources outside the school.

○ Engage students in designing the learning environment.

Continues on next page

Teaching
Standard **E** Teachers of science develop communities of science learners that reflect the intellectual rigor of scientific inquiry and the attitudes and social values conducive to science learning. In doing this, teachers

● **Display and demand respect for the diverse ideas, skills, and experiences of all students.**

○ Enable students to have a significant voice in decisions about the content and context of their work and require students to take responsibility for the learning of all members of the community.

○ Nurture collaboration among students.

○ Structure and facilitate ongoing formal and informal discussion based on a shared understanding of rules of scientific discourse.

● **Model and emphasize the skills, attitudes, and values of scientific inquiry.**

---

* Bold faced statements are discussed in the chapter.

Reprinted with permission from the *National Science Education Standards.* ©1996 National Academy of Sciences. Courtesy of the National Academy Press, Washington, DC.

Using Your Community Resources

The world of education places importance on communities' being involved with their local schools for good reason: Children, and adolescents in particular, need to feel they are an important and integral part of the communities in which they live. School and community partnerships fulfill a development need that cannot be satisfied by teachers alone. If only for this reason, forging those partnerships is a good idea.

But there is another good reason for using the resources in your community, and, although at first it may seem self-serving, at its heart is the support and promotion of your school and quality education. The more the community sees and experiences the good things you are doing in your classrooms and schools, the more the community will be willing to support and defend you and your school when critics come calling. Often, teachers and schools take a closed-door approach to education, shutting out the rest of the world and attempting to teach their students in a vacuum. This practice creates two negative outcomes:

- Students feel disconnected from and sometimes even hostile toward their communities.
- Communities, conversely, feel disconnected from their local schools and sometimes even suspicious of those who work in their local schools.

These two problems are common, but heading off the negative feelings that sometimes exist between communities and schools is relatively simple. As a teacher, you can take the lead in creating a positive relationship. There are three easily accessed resources in your community you can work with to this end: parents, community members, and field trips.

Parents: Diamonds in the Rough

Your first and easiest stop in accessing community resources should be obvious: your students' parents. With a bit of probing, you will find they bring a wealth of knowledge about practically any science-related subject you can dream up. There's no secret to uncovering this resource: All you have to do is ask.

The best time to start mining parent resources is at the beginning of the year when you, your students, and their parents are in a natural period of getting to know one another. You will probably send a letter home to parents to introduce yourself and your expectations for the classroom, or you will provide the same introductory materials at an open house. Take a few moments to create a brief survey that parents can fill out and return. (See Appendix A, pp. 108 and 109, for sample survey and a letter of introduction.)

A clear, concise survey is not a burden for parents and gives them a sense of contribution to their child's education. To avoid inadvertently offending any parents, make sure there is something on the survey that every parent, regardless of socioeconomic status, can respond to positively. Some

SCiLINKS®
THE WORLD'S A CLICK AWAY

Topic: careers in science
Go to: www.scilinks.org
Code: HMS73

questions you might ask that encompass the abilities of all parents are

- If your employment schedule permits, would you occasionally be able to come to our science classroom and serve as a lab assistant assisting the teacher with lab set-up, lab supplies, and lab cleanup?
- Do you work in a job where you use science-related knowledge or problem-solving skills? If yes, please tell me about your job.
- Would you be willing to collect household items such as 2-liter bottles, tissue paper, and newspaper for use in our classroom lab?
- Have you traveled to a location where you saw naturally occurring wonders like volcanoes, geysers, and marine life? Would you be willing to come to our classroom to share your experience with us? If your answer is yes, please tell me a little bit about your experience.

The answers will leave you astounded at the resources you have at your fingertips. When the surveys come back, take a few minutes to read through them and organize them based on where you think each parent's contributions could fit. You will find that parents enjoy being part of the classroom experience and will enrich your curriculum for your students.

Parents can play many roles and contribute in many ways to your science classroom. Three possibilities follow, but as you organize the information from returned surveys, an even bigger array of possibilities will likely occur to you.

Career Exploration

The best way to make concrete the sometimes mysterious and abstract concepts you teach in science class is to provide students with a dose of real-world science that relates directly to a concept. An effective instructional method is to bring in a parent whose job relates directly to that concept. Make sure you provide the parent with a copy of the chapter or materials you have covered that relate to his or her career. This helps the parent tailor the discussion to what the students have been taught. The more the students learn about a parent's career, the more they will see doors open before them.

Vacations and Life Experiences

Nearly everyone takes pictures or home videos when they go on vacation, and nearly everyone loves to share those memories. If you are studying a particular phenomenon, whether it be natural or man-made, chances are one of your students' parents has seen it and has taken pictures or brought back mementos. Students, and young adolescents in particular, love the social aspect of sharing stories and experiences and will enjoy it when parents come into the classroom and share theirs. Keep this option in mind as you work through your curriculum for the year.

Much-Needed Lab Assistants

Many parents are ready and willing to help you teach their child science but have a limited science background. Never fear: These parents are just as much a resource as the mother who is a rocket scientist working for NASA. As you attempt to provide as many hands-on lab activities as possible to enrich the learning process for your students, you will find that managing lab supplies, getting lab equipment and materials set up in a limited amount of time, and providing ample assistance to special needs students during labs can be quite overwhelming. Parents willing to serve as your lab assistants can be an invaluable resource. They can set up equipment, replenish materials as they are depleted during the day, help special needs students read the lab and follow directions, or assist you with cleanup and storage of lab materials. Although your students may whine about

these tasks, most parents are more than happy to lend a helping hand if they have the free time.

Higher Education and Business Communities

When you are developing your plan for creating positive public relations between your classroom and your community, don't forget to consider the business members of your community and your local colleges and universities. Although they may not have children who attend your school, they are still probably concerned, from a community and business standpoint, that their future employees and students are being given a good, solid education.

Career Exploration

Much like the parents of your students, members of your business community who work in a science-related industry provide a great way to show your students real-world science at work. At the beginning of the school year, call the science-related businesses in your community and ask if they have employees who would speak to your students. Many larger companies have stipulations in employee contracts that require employees to give a certain number of hours to local schools or volunteer efforts. Larger companies also may have a designated public relations employee who works with school groups in this manner. You will be surprised at the wealth of career exploration resources you will find in your business community.

Professors and students from local colleges and universities can provide a unique insight into concepts and career paths. Ask them to speak to your class about the how-to specifics of science career choices.

Resources

In addition to providing speakers for your classroom, the science-related industries in your community may be able to provide you with material resources for labs that do not fit into your science department budget. These businesses also may be willing to sponsor your school's science class projects with direct funding or materials. Many nurseries, for example, will provide nursery stock for botany projects or school outdoor labs at no cost. Additionally, some colleges and universities have access to grants that would allow them to collaborate with you on a project and provide you with needed resources.

Becoming involved with your state and national professional education organizations is also helpful. The National Science Teachers Association and the National Middle School Association should be two of your first stops as you venture into the world of teacher resources and professional development. They can direct you to your state level affiliates as well as other groups and organizations whose purpose is to help you become a better teacher of science to your students.

Field Trips

Field trips are a great way to show your students science concepts from their textbooks in action, and your students generally will be very excited to move beyond the school building walls and into the world around them. Trips can take a great deal of planning and organization on your part—an overnight bus trip to the Chicago Museum of Science and Industry, for instance—but keep in mind that field trips can be short junkets just outside your classroom window. For example, take a trip to that field next to the school that is full of wildflowers and insect specimens during the spring.

Every field trip, big or small, has organizational details you must take care of prior to departure. This section will help you plan a successful trip and keep your fellow faculty members and the administration happy.

Good Planning

Timeline. Plan major field trips, a half day or longer, as soon as possible to allow time to inform students, parents, and other faculty who teach your students, as well as the administrative staff in your school, about the trip. In general, give parents and staff members at least five to six weeks notice. For field trips on school grounds during your class period, try to let your main office know at least 24 hours in advance. Remember that giving advance notice shows respect for fellow staff members and will eliminate misunderstandings and frustrations.

Possible Destinations. The possibilities for field trips are endless. Some tried and true locations:

- Museums
- Zoos
- Aquariums
- Planetariums
- Farms
- Local/state/national parks
- Nurseries
- Lakes/rivers/oceanfront
- Factories/laboratories/hospitals
- School grounds, fields, wooded areas, neighborhood walks

Organization. There are two essential items you need to gather from students before you board the school bus for a field trip:

- Written permission from parents (see Appendix A, p. 110, for sample form)
- Any money or fees necessary for the field trip

Activities. Making sure students stay involved in a field trip is important. A field trip where students simply follow a docent around a museum in a lecture-style tour is not going to be successful. However, a few, simple ideas will help keep the students involved and engaged and out of trouble.

- Scavenger Hunt: Plan a scavenger hunt through a museum or zoo. This may require

that you visit the site prior to the field trip to put together questions and clues, but will be well worth the time. Most field trip destinations offer free or reduced costs to educators who want to visit before they bring their students. Be sure to ask about this.

- Alphabet Tour: Have students carry a notebook with them and write one word for each letter of the alphabet that is related to the field trip. Students should also write one sentence for each word to explain its relevance.
- Thumbnail Tour: Have the students carry drawing paper with them and sketch thumbnail drawings of the things they see. You can guide the drawings by giving instructions such as, "Draw a sketch of something organic you saw on the field trip." Using vocabulary terms from past science lessons extends the value of the field trip even farther.
- Post–Field Trip Quiz: Inform the students prior to departing they will have a post–field trip quiz when they return to school and it will be an open notes quiz. Allow students to take notes while on the field trip and use them during the quiz.
- Post–Field Trip Essay: Like the post–field trip quiz, students will take notes, but then will be asked to write a descriptive essay about the trip and the things they learned.

Assessing/Evaluating. Although giving students a letter grade for field trips is not necessary, evaluating them in some way is a good idea. This helps you determine the value of the field trip and makes it something more than just a social outing. Many field trip destinations will provide teachers with worksheets and pre– and post–field trip activities for use in the classroom.

Tell Everyone

In addition to parents, certain important people in your school must be notified about your field

trip plans. Make sure you inform them as far in advance as you can.

School Nurse. The school nurse or aide can provide you with a first-aid kit to take with you, as well as any medications your students will need during the day. If you are taking a large number of special needs students with you, the nurse or aide may even attend the field trip with your group.

Cafeteria Staff. Your cafeteria staff depends on a certain number of mouths to feed every day in order to maintain a healthy budget and pay its workers. Make sure you tell them when you are going to be pulling more than a few students out of lunch so they can plan their food preparation accordingly. In addition, if you are planning a field trip where students need a sack lunch, your cafeteria might be able to prepare them and have them ready to go when you board the bus.

Administrators. You should always get permission for a field trip idea from your administrators before beginning planning, and don't forget to invite them to attend the field trip with you. Many times they would enjoy a day out of the building with you and your students.

Other Teachers. Few things are more frustrating than spending hours planning a day's lesson only to find out at the last minute that half of your students are going to miss your class. Give the teachers with whom you share students advance notice so they can plan accordingly.

Parents. You will more than likely need parents as chaperones, so let them know when and where you will be going as soon as possible. That way, parents who work can make arrangements to change shifts or have the day off.

Take These With You

Your other essential planning task is to make sure you have emergency items ready to go. Here is a list of "must haves" for field trips:

- Emergency phone numbers for each child
- Medications and proper instructions for each child
- A cell phone or school radio
- A first-aid kit
- A map from your school to the field trip location —good in case you get lost, and copies can be given to parents who may be driving separately
- A couple of bottles of water and some snacks such as crackers and fruit for any diabetics on the trip
- A change of clothes—sweatpants and a T-shirt or sweatshirt work well—that would fit any of your students in case of an accident

With some planning and organization, field trips can be rewarding for you and your students. Keep an open mind about taking your students away from their desks and into the fascinating world of science around them, whether you are planning an overnight excursion to destinations far away or just a 40-minute class period in the school's football field. Your students will love it, and, although you might be a little tired at the end of the day, you will enjoy yourself too.

Resources

Professional Associations

National Science Teachers Association (*www.nsta.org*)
1840 Wilson Boulevard
Arlington, VA 22201-3000
703-243-7100

National Middle School Association (*www.nmsa.org*)
4151 Executive Parkway, Suite 300
Westerville, OH 43081
1-800-528-NMSA

CHAPTER
11

Periodical

Science Scope, a journal for middle and junior high school science teachers, available through the National Science Teachers Association by becoming an NSTA member. See preceding "Professional Associations."

Web Source URLs

Please note that websites are often changed, deleted, and moved.

Website	Subject
www.schoolgrants.org	grant clearinghouse and tips for grant-writing
www.eschoolnews.com/resources/funding	daily grant and funding sources
www.ed.gov/funding.html	U.S. Department of Education site for federal funding opportunities

National Science Education Standards Note:

*This chapter specifically addresses Teaching Standard A, bullet point two, and Teaching Standard D, bullet point five.

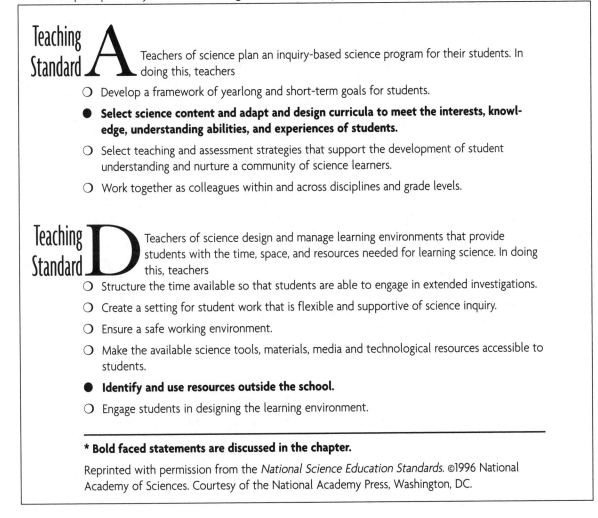

Teaching Standard A

Teachers of science plan an inquiry-based science program for their students. In doing this, teachers

○ Develop a framework of yearlong and short-term goals for students.

● **Select science content and adapt and design curricula to meet the interests, knowledge, understanding abilities, and experiences of students.**

○ Select teaching and assessment strategies that support the development of student understanding and nurture a community of science learners.

○ Work together as colleagues within and across disciplines and grade levels.

Teaching Standard D

Teachers of science design and manage learning environments that provide students with the time, space, and resources needed for learning science. In doing this, teachers

○ Structure the time available so that students are able to engage in extended investigations.

○ Create a setting for student work that is flexible and supportive of science inquiry.

○ Ensure a safe working environment.

○ Make the available science tools, materials, media and technological resources accessible to students.

● **Identify and use resources outside the school.**

○ Engage students in designing the learning environment.

***

* Bold faced statements are discussed in the chapter.

Reprinted with permission from the *National Science Education Standards.* ©1996 National Academy of Sciences. Courtesy of the National Academy Press, Washington, DC.

Teaming

By now, we hope you're feeling more comfortable about teaching science to middle school students. You're going to get the ball rolling in the right direction the first week using some great icebreakers from Chapter 2. You're ready to fascinate and inspire your students with safe and well-prepared lab lessons from Chapters 4 through 9. You've polished up your management skills with Chapter 10 and are ready to involve parents and the school community in your classroom with Chapter 11.

But, just when your confidence level reaches a high-water mark, your school administrator informs you you're part of an interdisciplinary team. You begin to wonder what teaming is all about and how it will affect the way you teach science.

The goal of this chapter is to give you a brief overview of the purpose of teaming and highlight how it can be a positive addition to your middle school students' overall learning experience. Numerous resources explain teaming and offer suggestions for teams just forming as well as veteran teams that need rejuvenation (see Resources). The bottom line is that teaming is not a concept to be feared or resented, but rather one that will make your subject area seem more real world for your students than if it had to stand alone.

To give you the background you need to be a contributing member of your team, let's start with the basics.

What Is Teaming?

Teaming is a method of grouping students so they share the same set of teachers for their core subject areas—science, math, language arts, social studies, and sometimes physical education and health. Most often, teams are created when an entire grade is broken into groups who share the same set of teachers. Small schools that do not have enough students to form teams can create a grade-level team or multigrade-level teams. The core subject teachers usually share a common planning period and, in many situations, also share a team planning period. Teaming is most often used in middle grades education because its positive outcomes are particularly appropriate to the developmental needs of young adolescents. One study of middle grades schools found "over 90 percent of the schools deemed 'exemplary' in one study were organized into teams." This same study "also concluded that [with teaming] students learn more, behave better, feel more positive about schools and teachers, and interact better with each other, even if the school represents two or more sizable ethnic groups." (Arnold and Stevenson 1998)

Teaming Goals

Teaming has four outcomes that make educational experts feel it is a worthwhile instructional method for young adolescents.

The "Big Fish" Theory. One of the most important developmental needs of young adolescents is

that they have a sense of belonging and personal identity within a group. By breaking large groups of students into smaller ones, a student can go from being a small fish in a big pond to a big fish in a small pond. The outcome with teams is that students know each other better, feel like their teachers know them better, and don't feel lost in the crowd.

Individual Attention/Early Intervention. When a group of teachers shares the same students all day, it is easier for teachers to catch problems—or successes—early on to make sure they are recognized and dealt with properly. The team teachers communicate on a daily basis and can compare and contrast individual student behaviors to determine how best to serve a student's needs. Because they can catch behaviors as soon as they start, teachers can refer students for special services sooner, inform parents of concerns sooner, and head off many problems before they take root. Students, knowing their teachers are working as a team, realize they are more accountable for their choices than if they were left to float among individual teachers who never communicated with one another until a serious situation developed.

Scheduling Flexibility, Team Activities, Personal/ Social Relationships. Because all of the students and team teachers share the same schedule each day, teaming makes flexible schedules possible. For example, if you have planned a dissection lab, it may take longer than 45 minutes for your students to complete. Rather than bagging the specimen and hoping it keeps until the next day, a flexed schedule might allow you to have your science classes last 60, or even 90, minutes while other classes are shortened for that day. In addition, this common schedule allows you and your teammates to plan for special activities such as field trips, team-building activities, and spe-cial speakers with minimal disruptions to the rest of the staff in your building. And, finally, sharing the same schedule day in and day out gives students opportunities to build social relationships with their peers, an extremely important need in healthy adolescent development.

Integrating Curriculum/Interdisciplinary Teaching. Perhaps the most underused advantage of teaming lies in opportunities for integration of curriculum and the development of interdisciplinary units. Sharing the same students and the same daily schedule allows team teachers to discuss their subject curriculums and recognize where they overlap. Although we commonly recognize the subjects we teach are intertwined, we still sometimes teach as if we are in a vacuum. With teaming, teachers can share with one another the goings-on in their classrooms and identify concepts and subjects that overlap. The overlaps can then be pointed out to the students so they can see the dependency one subject has on other subjects they are required to take.

Team Characteristics

Often, teams of teachers will share a planning period. They use these times to plan for team activities, discuss student concerns, hold parent conferences, meet with administrators and support staff, and design and develop integrated and interdisciplinary curriculums.

Usually, one of the characteristics of a middle school team is a group identity. Many teams adopt names, mottos, colors, or mascots. This helps distinguish one team from another and develops further the big-fish-in-a-small-pond feeling.

Teams of teachers often plan activities the entire team will do as a group. Those activities help cultivate life skills learning, social skills development, and teamwork and leadership qualities as well as enhance the academic enrichment engen-

dered by interdisciplinary units and integrated curriculum. They are aimed at helping each student feel part of the group and form positive relationships with peers as well as with teachers.

Interdisciplinary Units

One of the biggest myths about interdisciplinary units is that a unit must involve all core subject teachers to count as interdisciplinary. That is not true. An interdisciplinary unit involves simply two or more teachers who develop a unit of study based around the same theme, topic, or general concept to show students how the subjects interrelate in regard to that topic. Generally, interdisciplinary units are planned in advance and are carried out as stand-alone time periods—anywhere from a few days to a couple of weeks—outside of the regular curriculum when the team teachers deem it most appropriate. For example, a team may do a unit of study on baseball in the fall when the World Series is taking place.

Integrated Curriculum

Curriculum integration, unlike interdisciplinary units, generally is done throughout the year and within the regular curriculum. In simple terms, curriculum integration is the reinforcement and integration of other subject areas within your own subject area on a regular basis. For example, as a science teacher, you may require your students to figure their own percentage grades out of the points they earn on assignments to reinforce the process of finding percentages they learn in math class. Or, whenever you assign a formal lab write-up, you may insist your students use proper grammar and spelling to reinforce the concepts learned in language arts class. Curriculum integration is not difficult on a basic level if you and your fellow team teachers communicate to one another the key concepts and skills being taught and emphasized in each of the classes.

What Does Science Have to Do With Teaming?

You are in luck. Science is perhaps the easiest class to fit into the teaming concept. The vast array of topics covered, the numerous skills your students will learn, and the natural interest young adolescents have in science will help your subject be a catalyst for many positive team experiences. Here are several springboard ideas for interdisciplinary units and curriculum integration to help you brainstorm how science can be part of your team's activities.

Historical Perspectives. Studying famous scientists or famous scientific discoveries works particularly well with social studies classes. Possibilities include Albert Einstein, the race to the Moon, and Newton's laws.

Biology. Life forms and life processes can be quite interesting units of study. These units work well with language arts classes, physical education and health classes, and related arts classes. Possibilities include the circle of life, the systems of the body, and death and dying.

Weather. Weather, because we all deal with it on a daily basis, is a real-world topic for students. Related units combine well with math classes, language arts classes, and physical education and health classes. Possibilities include weather disasters, the water cycle, and the changing seasons.

Physics. Physical science with all its formulas and theories can be dry and intimidating for students. However, combined with other subjects, particularly math, the whole fascinating world of physics can come alive for young adolescents. Possibilities include boat design/construction/racing, bridges and architecture, and the world of motion.

Space/Astronomy. Almost all young adolescents find space science fascinating. Math and language arts fit well into these units of study. Possibilities include flight, constellations, and the solar system.

Chemistry. Chemistry is one of the more difficult science subjects to integrate, but it can be done. Keep in mind historical perspectives and mathematical relationships when attempting to use chemistry in interdisciplinary units. Possibilities include the elements, medicine and pharmacology, and biochemistry.

Earth Science. This is perhaps the easiest subject to use as a springboard for interdisciplinary units. Almost any topic within Earth science integrates with many other subjects in a meaningful way. Possibilities include creating your own island, natural disasters, and agriculture.

Bringing Science into Other Subjects

Sometimes, your teammates may be excited about an interdisciplinary unit that seems to have no relationship to science at all. But there are ways to integrate your subject into those units, at least on a minimal level, often through labs.

Your goal as a science teacher should always be to find ways to involve your students in their studies through hands-on methods. This is also a good goal for tough-to-integrate units. Your labs can be as simple as growing and observing different types of grass during a baseball unit.

A good place to find simple labs for your students to do during these units is their textbooks from other subjects. Many textbook companies now include supplements for integrating curriculum and will include labs in social studies, health, math, and even language arts books. If you are not sure where to find these supplemental materials, ask your teammates or your school's media specialist.

Some other suggestions:

Don't Forget the Past. Too often, a middle grades science curriculum does not allow much time to study the contributions of past scientists to the vast knowledge we have today. If the unit you are trying to be part of involves study of a specific time period, or a specific part of the world, have the students research a person from that time or location who made a contribution to the world of science.

There's Always a Problem to Be Solved. In almost any unit of study, there either is, or was, a problem to be solved. Have your science students show you how the scientific method was—or should have been—used to solve that problem. Interdisciplinary units can be a wonderful way for you to revisit the scientific method with your students and show them how it applies to any problem a human being faces.

Staying Flexible

Perhaps the most important quality you will need to have—or develop if you don't have it yet—is flexibility. The quickest way to ruin all the positive outcomes of the teaming concept is with a team member who is inflexible and unwilling to give a little to his or her colleagues. It is easy to go into our classrooms, close the door, and think we teach our beloved science in a vacuum. Instead, we must remember we are only a small part of the overall education our students deserve, rich not only in science, but many other fascinating and equally important subjects. If you can keep that in mind as you work with your teammates, give a little when you can see something is very important to a colleague, and find ways to integrate your subject with the others your students experience each day, you will find teaming a pleasant experience for you and your students.

The second most important thing for keeping your team healthy and student-centered is good communication and record keeping. When you meet as a team, designate someone as record keeper. Make sure that person writes a description of anything discussed, any decisions made, and any ac-

tions to be taken and by whom. This will help your team get things done in a timely manner and create a paper trail that may come in handy when a parent or another school staff member has questions about students or team activities. (See Appendix A, p. 111, for a sample "team log" sheet.)

As in any professional relationship, it is important your team keep other school staff members apprised of what is happening with your team. Make sure administrators, guidance counselors, support staff, and nonteam faculty members are aware of team activities and any student concerns that may affect them as soon as possible. Good communication between your team and the rest of your school will help make the positive outcomes of teaming more effective.

Finally, it is important that each faculty member of your team has a role and specific responsibilities to make sure the teaming process is smooth and productive. You can determine these roles and responsibilities for the specific needs of your students and school, but we strongly encourage the following be represented in some way on your team:

Team Leader—sets the team meeting agendas, keeps the group on task, serves as liaison to administration. This position is often appointed by your principal and, in some schools, is a paid assignment.

Team Secretary—keeps the daily team log, handles team paperwork

School Relations Liaison—works with guidance counselors, special education, related arts, and support staff when appropriate

Public Relations Liaison—works with parents and also organizes submissions for school newsletters and local newspapers

Team Treasurer—organizes and tracks money designated for team, making sure deadlines are met

and orders are submitted properly and in a timely manner

Teaming, although it can be overwhelming at first, is a wonderful way for your students to begin to see how, in the real world, they will take the individual, compartmentalized subjects they learn in school and blend them to create a functional and fascinating society. Students will appreciate how teaming gives them a sense of belonging and how it answers the age-old question, "What do I need to know this for?" Parents will appreciate how teaming helps a teacher find and recognize concerns or successes, giving students a much more individualized education. And, with a little flexibility and common sense when it comes to communication, you will appreciate the creative freedom teaming gives you and your colleagues as you work to develop well-rounded, thoughtful students in each of your classes.

References

Arnold, J., and C. Stevenson. 1998. *Teachers' teaming handbook: A middle level planning guide.* Fort Worth, Texas: Harcourt Brace College Publishers.

Resources

Book/Print Sources

Forte, I., and S. Schurr. 1996. *Integrating instruction in science: Strategies, activities, projects, tools, & techniques.* Nashville, TN: Incentive Publications, Inc. ISBN# 0-86530-321-5 (activities, projects, and integration techniques)

Rottier, J. 2001. *Implementing and improving teaming.* Westerville, OH: NMSA Publications. ISBN# 156090-166-7 (teaming handbook for middle grades teachers)

Periodicals

Science Scope (journal for middle and junior high school science teachers) through the National Science Teachers Association by becoming an NSTA member. (NSTA, 1840 Wilson Boulevard, Arlington, Virginia 22201-3000, 703.243.7100. www.nsta.org)

CHAPTER
12

National Science Education Standards Note:

*This chapter specifically addresses Teaching Standard A, bullet point four, and Teaching Standard C, bullet points four and five.

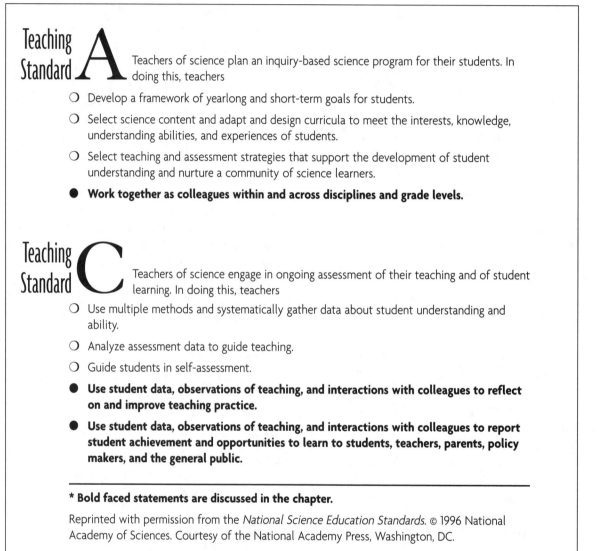

Teaching Standard A

Teachers of science plan an inquiry-based science program for their students. In doing this, teachers

○ Develop a framework of yearlong and short-term goals for students.

○ Select science content and adapt and design curricula to meet the interests, knowledge, understanding abilities, and experiences of students.

○ Select teaching and assessment strategies that support the development of student understanding and nurture a community of science learners.

● **Work together as colleagues within and across disciplines and grade levels.**

Teaching Standard C

Teachers of science engage in ongoing assessment of their teaching and of student learning. In doing this, teachers

○ Use multiple methods and systematically gather data about student understanding and ability.

○ Analyze assessment data to guide teaching.

○ Guide students in self-assessment.

● **Use student data, observations of teaching, and interactions with colleagues to reflect on and improve teaching practice.**

● **Use student data, observations of teaching, and interactions with colleagues to report student achievement and opportunities to learn to students, teachers, parents, policy makers, and the general public.**

* Bold faced statements are discussed in the chapter.

Reprinted with permission from the *National Science Education Standards*. © 1996 National Academy of Sciences. Courtesy of the National Academy Press, Washington, DC.

Substitute Teachers

Our daily lives are ones of certainty and surprise, yin and yang existences. Some things we can control and others we are powerless to command, even with the best intentions. Teachers are not exempt from emergencies, jury duty, and illness. Luckily, most schools plan for such incidents by having willing substitutes on hand. Teachers need to follow the Scout's motto of "be prepared" to keep the classroom running smoothly and efficiently for students and subs.

Just as in planning a lesson or unit, organization is the key to being prepared for inevitable absence. Invest in a sturdy folder or notebook, and label it clearly for substitute teacher use. Have this readily available in the classroom, and let other teachers—team leader, teacher next door, and/or department head—know where it is kept. It might be wise to buy tabs or dividers to mark clearly the various sections in this folder. Include the following items in this resource:

Seating charts and room assignments—list special needs students and any other adults that may be in the class such as an aide or team teacher. Make sure you update these charts any time changes are made.

Attendance procedures

Daily schedule—list class times and room assignments; lunch (where to get and eat lunch, lunch room prices, soda/snack machines, prep time, team time, and hall duty

Map of school—highlight room assignments, elevator access, faculty lounge, prep area, team/department area, office, clinic, library/media center, gymnasium, cafeteria, and any other area you think is useful

School phone book or list of extensions, if applicable

List of people—include those who can help with questions, problems, or incidents, such as team leader, teacher next door, and department head

Passes procedure—include student passes, hall passes, and clinic passes.

Emergency plans—clearly explain the procedures and exit routes. Also include location of classroom safety equipment such as fire extinguisher, eye wash, shower, and fire blanket.

Lesson plans—whether in the plan book, phoned in to a fellow teacher, secretary, or administrator, or found in a folder of activities to do in case of an emergency, these are crucial. Even though most subs are highly qualified and very capable, it may be a good idea to postpone a lab or other hands-on activity and submit something else instead for the day.

Directions for using video player, television, remote, computer

Thank you—if the absence is a planned one, include a thank-you note on the lesson plan or change for a soda

(See Appendix A, p. 112, for a quick reference, bulleted list.)

Preparing Students

Now the grunt work has been organized into a notebook, the next step is to make students aware of why you could be absent and your expectations for when you are. Explain the various reasons—

illness, emergencies, death, family crisis, accidents—many of which students can relate to, and that class will continue with the help of a substitute teacher. Discuss the word "substitute" and help students realize that, although this person is not the regular classroom teacher, he or she is qualified by the school district to substitute teach.

Tell students the substitute will not know how the class is usually run or have the same personality or tolerance level as you and that they must act in a mature, respectful manner. Be very clear about your expectations. For example, tell your students you expect the substitute to report to you that the students were "nothing less than angelic." Setting high expectations and being extremely serious about them will help instill in students how important their behavior with the substitute teacher is. Although they may not reach an angelic level, chances are good most will be on their best-possible behavior.

Learning takes place and, except for minor interruptions dealing with change, the classroom continues to function smoothly when substitute planning is viewed as another aspect of classroom preparation.

When You Return

When you return, be prepared for a substitute report. These remarks can be quite lengthy with every minute detail spelled out or as simple as checkmarks made in the lesson plans. If there are items you want the sub to tell you, prepare a sub report checklist (see Appendix A, p. 113) and indicate its use in the sub folder. Students may also report on how things went. Address issues or concerns from sub or students as you see fit. If anything was threatening, damaging, or illegal, report it immediately to an administrator or supervisor. If the sub did an exemplary job, report this to the sub director, administrator, or supervisor, and write the sub's name down so you can ask for that person the next time. If the sub did not follow lesson plans or left the room in a shambles, tell the powers that be and note that name, too, so you can ask not to have that person.

If you see a sub in the building, know a sub will be stepping in for a team or department member, or notice a sub standing outside the room next door, take a moment to greet him or her. If the opportunity arises, check with the sub during the day to see how everything is going. Not only will the sub appreciate it, but the absent teacher will, too.

The End?

The end? Hardly. Teaching is an ongoing process. Rather than being a reflection of any single style, teaching is a combination of methods and real-life applications. Teachers must incorporate a variety of instructional techniques, find new insights for problem solving, and demonstrate there are numerous ways to learn. This involves time, research and learning, and adjusting to change.

When you first begin teaching, it can seem the days are longer than 24 hours, filled with planning, meetings, grading, researching, creating, supervising, duties, managing—and, oh yes, teaching. It is our hope that after the first year you will learn how to cope with that feeling of being overwhelmed—you get used to it in teaching. Don't take that as a condemnation of the profession. Rather, it is one of the things that keeps the job challenging and lively. Another is that classroom of new and eager faces you will see each year.

Another fact you will learn in the teaching years to come is that your learning continues. Most of us have heard and used the phrase "the importance of lifelong learning" without much thought about what that really means. In creating this resource book, for example, we have learned much about the world of publishing—experiencing the process involved in getting published, accepting the gentle as well as the rough criticism of the work, and making changes and additions per suggestions of reviewers and editors. We have also discovered new points about teaching science and are anxious to give them a go in the classroom this fall.

This brings us to an oxymoron in our career choice—constant change. Yes, education, like many other professions, is in a state of steady instability. In Chapter 3, you read that the *Atlas of Science Literacy* framework will change as educational research continues. This will affect you as a teacher, too. In our years of experience, we have continued to change and evolve as educators. We often wish we could bring back the students we had during the first couple of years of our teaching to show them what we can do now.

The first year of teaching is full of many experiences, both successes and failures. You will likely find that summer break comes up on you suddenly, and you'll catch yourself thinking, "What now?"

Challenge yourself to continue to grow and develop as a teacher of science. Teaching Standard F from the National Science Education Standards says, in part, that teachers of science should "participate fully in planning and implementing professional growth and development strategies for themselves and their colleagues" (NRC 1996).

The summer is a great time to rejuvenate yourself, not only personally, but also professionally, before a new school year begins. You will find many organizations and associations host professional development opportunities during the summer months that can help you keep your teaching repertoire fresh and up to date with the latest in best practices.

There are three great places to look for quality professional development experiences during the

summer. First, get in touch with your state-level National Science Teachers Association affiliate. (Visit *www.nsta.org* to locate your state affiliate.) Second, get in touch with your state-level National Middle School Association affiliate. (Visit *www.nmsa.org* to locate your state affiliate.) And finally, make contact with your state's Department of Education science education specialist to find out what opportunities await you during the summer months.

As well, don't forget all the fine published resources available to science teachers and teachers of middle grades in general. Both NSTA and NMSA publish outstanding books that will be invaluable resources for you as you venture from novice to master teacher over the next few years. (Visit the two websites in the above paragraph to find book lists and ordering information.) Just a few of these titles are listed in Appendix C, but countless others are available to assist you in your journey.

We hope this book has been a help to you as you traveled through your first year. It was our intention to introduce you to some key concepts and help you tackle them with added confidence to find success in your classroom. Now you must take the concepts you have begun to experiment with and do further, in-depth, study to expand your abilities as a teacher of middle grades science.

As you journey forward from your first year, remember all the things you have learned, and never forget to continue learning. And next year on the first day of school when you see a rookie teacher walking down the hall with that all-too-familiar bewildered look, make sure you stop and offer your help. You're on your way to being a pro now.

As we clearly stated in Chapter 1, our motivation was to give you some help in starting off that first year of teaching science, and the rest was up to you. But remember you are not alone. You have colleagues, team members, department chair people, mentors, administrators, and us. If you have questions, need additional information, seek help, or just want to let us know how your first year is going, please contact us at C74j78s84@aol.com or mssteward@msn.com.

Good luck! We know you will do your best, and that is all anyone can ask.

Resource

Book/Print Sources

National Research Council. 1996. *National Science Education Standards.* Washington, DC: National Academy Press. Online version at: books.nap.edu/books/0309053269/html/index.html

Tests and Forms

Can You Follow Directions?

This is a timed test. You have two minutes and 43 seconds.

1. Read everything carefully before doing anything.
2. Put your name in the upper right-hand corner of this paper.
3. Circle the word "name" in sentence two.
4. Draw five small squares in the upper left-hand corner.
5. Put an "X" in each square.
6. Put a circle around each square.
7. Sign your name under the title of this paper.
8. After the title, write "yes, yes, yes."
9. Put a circle completely around sentence number seven.
10. Put an "X" in the lower left corner of this paper.
11. Draw a triangle around the "X" you just put down.
12. Draw a rectangle around the word "corner" in sentence four.
13. On the back of this paper, multiply 705 by 66.
14. Loudly call out your first name when you get this far along.
15. If you think you have followed directions carefully up to this point, shout, "I HAVE!"
16. On the reverse side of this paper, add 8990 and 9805.
17. Put a circle around your answer, and then put a square around the circle.
18. In your normal speaking voice, count from one to ten, backwards.
19. Punch three small holes in the top of this paper, using the pen or pencil point.
20. Underline all even numbers on the left side of this paper.
21. Put a square around each written number on this page.
22. Loudly call out "I AM THE LEADER, AND I HAVE FOLLOWED DIRECTIONS".
23. Now that you have finished reading everything carefully, do only sentences one and two.

Science Lab Safety Rules

Always wash your hands before and after experiments.

Read all directions for an experiment carefully before beginning. Follow all directions exactly as written or explained by the teacher.

Never perform unauthorized activities.

Never mix chemicals or other materials for the fun of it.

Maintain a clean work area.

When an experiment is completed, always clean up the work area and return equipment to its proper place.

Never eat in lab unless authorized to do so.

Know the location of safety equipment in the lab and how to use it.

Always wear safety goggles when working with chemicals, burners, or any substance or object that might injure eyes.

Wear a lab apron when working with chemicals, burners, and other hazardous materials.

Keep all lids closed when a chemical is not being used.

Many chemicals and hazardous materials are poisonous. Never touch, taste, or smell any chemical. If instructed to smell the fumes in an experiment, gently wave a hand over the opening of the container and direct the fumes toward the nose.

Dispose of all chemicals and materials as instructed by the teacher.

Take care not to spill any materials in lab. If a spill does occur, notify teacher for clean-up directions.

Be careful when working with acids and bases. Always wear protective gloves when using strong acids or bases. Always pour acid into water when diluting the acid. **NEVER** pour water into acid.

Rinse any acids or bases off skin or clothing with water.

Notify teacher of any acid or base spill.

Never reach across a flame.

Keep all materials not used in lab away from flame. Pull back long hair and push up long sleeves if necessary.

Always point a test tube or bottle being heated away from you and others.

Never heat liquid in a closed container.

Always use a clamp, tong, or heat-resistant mitts when handling hot containers.

Use a wire screen to protect glassware when heating.

● Never heat glassware that is not thoroughly dry.

Never use broken or chipped glassware. If glassware breaks, notify the teacher.

Notify the teacher immediately if you are cut in lab.

All sharps materials and broken glass are to be disposed of in the proper container.

The gas jets, strikers, and Bunsen burners are to be used properly, as well as any material used to create a flame.

Students are held accountable for their actions in lab. Breaking these rules could have serious consequences, one of which may be loss of lab privileges.

Laboratory Ticket

Name_____ **Period** _____ **Date** _____

Caught:

❑ Not wearing goggles

❑ Not wearing apron

❑ Not following lab directions

❑ Doing unauthorized activities during lab

❑ Not wearing protective gloves when working
    with hazardous chemicals or handling hot items

❑ Did not clean up lab area

❑ Other:

Consequence:

❑ Conference with student

❑ Discipline Log

❑ Phone call home

❑ Referral to counselor

❑ Point deduction on lab: 10% 15% 20%

❑ Conference with parent

❑ Dismissed from lab with assigned grade of "F"

❑ Referral to administrator

❑ Other:

Laboratory Ticket

Name_____ **Period** _____ **Date** _____

Caught:

❑ Not wearing goggles

❑ Not wearing apron

❑ Not following lab directions

❑ Doing unauthorized activities during lab

❑ Not wearing protective gloves when working
    with hazardous chemicals or handling hot items

❑ Did not clean up lab area

❑ Other:

Consequence:

❑ Conference with student

❑ Discipline Log

❑ Phone call home

❑ Referral to counselor

❑ Point deduction on lab: 10% 15% 20%

❑ Conference with parent

❑ Dismissed from lab with assigned grade of "F"

❑ Referral to administrator

❑ Other:

Lab Safety Quiz

Name _____**Period** _____

Circle the BEST answer.

1. To protect yourself from chemical splashes or other dangerous objects you should
   a. wear goggles
   b. stand back from the lab table
   c. wear goggles and an apron
   d. wear an apron

2. If your lab partner gets chemicals in his eyes, the first thing you should do is
   a. clean up the spilled chemical
   b. call 9-1-1
   c. take him to the eyewash station and tell the teacher immediately
   d. make the person sit down to calm his nerves

3. Animals that are used during labs, dead and alive, should NOT be
   a. mistreated
   b. abused in any way
   c. teased or tormented jokingly
   d. all of the above

4. When using scalpels, scissors, or other sharp objects in labs, you should
   a. cut toward yourself
   b. cut away from yourself
   c. cut anything you want to
   d. cut as quickly as possible

5. If you break glassware during a lab, you should
   a. clear people out of the area and tell the teacher immediately
   b. clear people out of the area and leave the broken glass for a janitor
   c. tell the teacher on the way out of class at the end of the period
   d. try to clean it up yourself quickly so you won't bother anyone else

6. Before you begin a lab, you should have
   a. read all the instructions
   b. asked for any clarification
   c. made sure you have all the lab materials you need
   d. all of the above

7. When heating a substance in a test tube, the test tube should be pointed
   a. away from you
   b. toward you
   c. away from you and others
   d. toward you and away from others

8. After using Bunsen burners in a lab, you should _____ before you leave the classroom.
   a. unhook the apparatus and store it
   b. turn off the gas supply
   c. both a and b are correct
   d. neither a nor b is correct

9. During a lab, it is okay to
   a. have a snack
   b. taste chemicals that are not dangerous
   c. take lab materials out of the classroom if you were going to throw them away anyway
   d. none of the above

(cont.)

Lab Safety Quiz (cont.)

10. When the lab is over, your lab station should
    a. have a clean and dry surface
    b. have clean and neatly stored equipment
    c. have all power sources and gas unplugged and turned off
    d. all of the above

True or False?
Mark "T" or "F" in the space provided.

_____ 11. You can run through the lab area as long as you are not using chemicals, fire, or sharp objects.

_____ 12. Lab glassware is fragile and can break easily.

_____ 13. People with long hair need to tie it back before doing a lab.

_____ 14. The hood should be used if you are heating substances that give off toxic fumes.

_____ 15. Broken glassware should be thrown away in the classroom trash can immediately.

_____ 16. Pour used lab chemicals back into the stock containers when you are done.

_____ 17. If you aren't using chemicals, you don't ever have to wear goggles or aprons.

_____ 18. When diluting an acid, pour the acid into the water.

_____ 19. You should only do activities that are authorized by your teacher.

_____ 20. If the lab directions tell you to smell fumes, it's okay to take a big sniff of them.

Answers

1. C   3. D   5. A   7. C   9. D   11. F   13. T   15. F   17. F   19. T
2. C   4. B   6. D   8. C   10. D   12. T   14. T   16. F   18. T   20. F

Fill-in-the-Blank Sample Rubric

Student's Name _____ Class Period _____ Date _____

Assignment Name _____

Section 1: Description of Tasks to Complete

Task 1: *Describe first objective.*

Rating: Excellent = Point Value _____

Describe everything that is expected to reach this value.

Rating: Good = Point Value _____

Describe everything that is expected to reach this value.

Rating: Average = Point Value _____

Describe everything that is expected to reach this value.

Rating: Poor = Point Value _____

Describe everything that is expected to reach this value.

Rating: Did not do = Point Value is zero.

Task 2-?: *Repeat the same steps for Task 1.*

Section 2: Task Scoring

Task 1: Score _____ Notes/Comments:

Task 2: Score _____ Notes/Comments:

Repeat for as many tasks as required

Section 3: Final Grade

Total Points Earned _____ / Total Points Possible _____ = **Final Percentage Grade** _____

Final Letter Grade _____

Lab Report Format

Heading _____

Name of Scientist _____

Date of Experiment _____

Location of Experiment _____

Title of Lab

Purpose/Objective: *Explain why you are doing this lab. What do you want to find out? (1–2 sentences)*

Prediction/Hypothesis: *What do you think the outcome of this lab will be? (1–2 sentences)*

Materials Needed: *List the materials you need for this lab. Be specific!*

Procedure: *List, in order, the steps you will follow to complete this lab.*

Data Collected/Observations: *Use this section to write down measurements, observations made, and other information you are required to collect as you perform the lab.*

Charts/Graphs: *Use this section to show any charts or graphs you created from the data you collected in the previous section.*

Conclusion: *Write a paragraph explaining the outcome of the lab. Include in this paragraph if your hypothesis was right or wrong. If it was wrong, explain why. Explain what you learned from this lab and if you met the initial objective. Finally, if this lab leads you to more questions (things you'd like to find out through another lab) make sure those questions are included as well.*

The Standard Measurement Quiz

Convert the following:

1. 32 ounces = _____ pints

2. 120 grains = _____ drams

3. 16 quarts = _____ pecks

4. 1 barrel = _____ gallons

5. 80 rods = _____ furlongs

6. 12 miles = _____ leagues

7. 1 scruple = _____ grains

8. 1 ounce = _____ pennyweights

9. Name at least four units of measure for liquid volume.

   a. _____   c. _____
   b. _____   d. _____

10. Name at least four units of measure for weight.

    a. _____   c. _____
    b. _____   d. _____

11. Find the cost of 42 feet of wire if it costs 92¢ a yard.

12. There are 1,760 yards in a mile. How many inches are in one mile?

The Standard Measurement Quiz

ANSWERS

1. 32 ounces = _____2_____ pints

2. 120 grains = _____2_____ drams

3. 16 quarts = _____2_____ pecks

4. 1 barrel = _____31–42_____ gallons

5. 80 rods = _____2_____ furlongs

6. 12 miles = _____4_____ leagues

7. 1 scruple = _____20_____ grains

8. 1 ounce = _____20_____ pennyweights

9. Name at least four units of measure for liquid volume.

   answers will vary

   a._____ c._____

   b._____ d._____

10. Name at least four units of measure for weight.

    answers will vary

    a._____ c._____

    b._____ d._____

11. Find the cost of 42 feet of wire if it costs 92¢ a yard.

    $12.88

12. There are 1,760 yards in a mile. How many inches are in one mile?

    63,360

Stair-Step Conversion Method

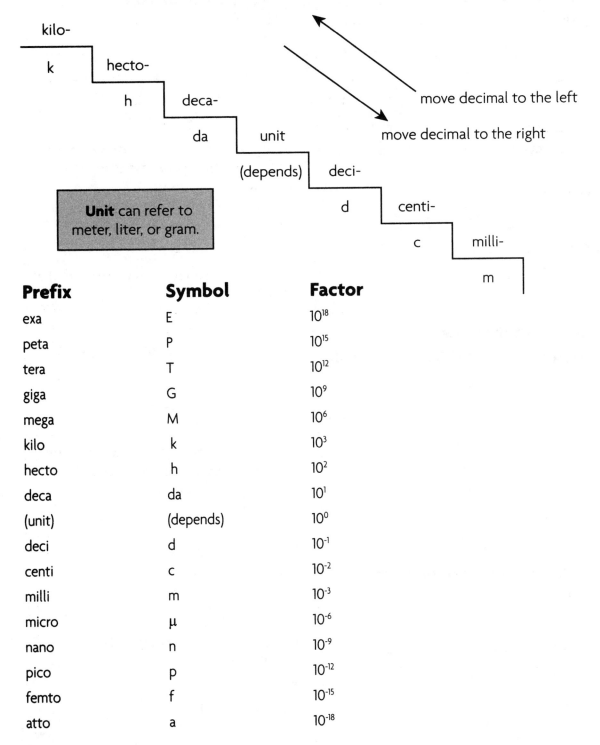

move decimal to the left

move decimal to the right

Unit can refer to meter, liter, or gram.

Prefix	Symbol	Factor
exa	E	10^{18}
peta	P	10^{15}
tera	T	10^{12}
giga	G	10^{9}
mega	M	10^{6}
kilo	k	10^{3}
hecto	h	10^{2}
deca	da	10^{1}
(unit)	(depends)	10^{0}
deci	d	10^{-1}
centi	c	10^{-2}
milli	m	10^{-3}
micro	μ	10^{-6}
nano	n	10^{-9}
pico	p	10^{-12}
femto	f	10^{-15}
atto	a	10^{-18}

SI Worksheet

Complete this table:

Unit	Symbol	Measure
Celsius	_____	temperature
_____	m	length, distance
_____	g	mass
_____	_____	fluid volume
cubic centimeters	cm^3 or cc	solid volume

Define:

mass _____

volume _____

temperature _____

Complete the table:

Prefix	Symbol	Value
_____	k	1000
_____	h	_____
deca-	_____	_____
_____	_____	.1
_____	c	.01
_____	milli-	.001

Write out the meaning of the symbols:

mm = _____

dL = _____

hg = _____

Write the symbols for the following:

decaliter _____

kilometer _____

centigram _____

Answer these questions based on SI prefixes and their meanings:

If a centipede has as many legs as its name implies (it does not, though), each leg is what part of the total number of legs?

In a millennium, each year is what part of the total period of time?

A decade is a period of _____ years.

A hectoacre has _____ metric acres.

A kilowatt equals _____ watts.

Using the formulas given, convert the temperatures in the problems.

$°C = (°F − 32) ÷ 1.8$ $°F = (°C \times 1.8) + 32$ $K = °C + 273.15$

21°C = _____ °F

672 °F = _____ °C

7 °C = _____ K

*143 °F = _____ K

Complete the following metric conversions:

56 dam = ____ cm

14.356 mg = ____ hg

12 kL = ____ L

Science Lab Instruments

Draw the temperature that is indicated on each of the thermometers below. The unit is °C.

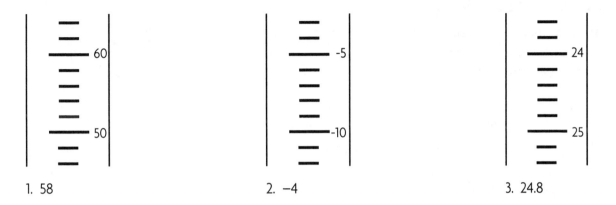

1. 58

2. −4

3. 24.8

Draw the volume that is indicated on each of the graduated containers below.

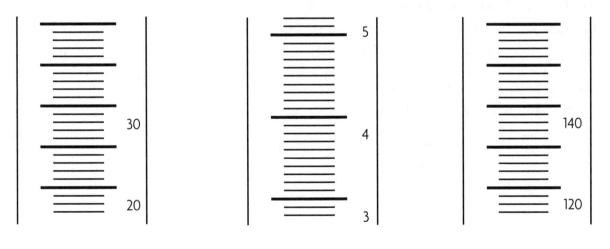

4.   27 mL

5. 4.2 mL

6. 129 mL

Draw a triple beam balance diagram to indicate a mass of 593.7 g.

Measurement Work Stations

Name _____

STATION 1: Using a balance

Instructions: Use the balance to determine the mass of each of the items at the station. Place object on balance tray. Follow posted directions to use balance. Total the mass indicators and record the mass in grams (g).

Item   **Mass**

STATION 2: Using a graduated cylinder

Instructions: Use the graduated cylinder to determine the volume of each container. Fill the container with water and pour it into the graduated cylinder. Observe the upper surface of the water in the graduated cylinder is curved or crescent-shaped. This curved surface is called the **meniscus** (me-nis-cuss). When measuring a volume of liquid, always visually line up with the bottom of the meniscus. Read the amount on the cylinder and record the volume in mL.

Container #   **Volume**

STATION 3: Using a Celsius thermometer

Instructions: Use a Celsius thermometer to record the temperature. Place the thermometer in the beaker of ice water and record the temperature readings, in °C, every minute for 3 minutes.

Minute   **Temperature**

Instructions: Use a Celsius thermometer to record the temperature. Place the thermometer in the beaker of hot water and record the temperature readings, in ºC, every minute for three minutes.

Minute	Temperature

STATION 4: Using a metric ruler to determine solid volume

Instructions: Use a metric ruler to determine the volume of each illustration below. Record the length, width, and height (in cm), then multiply to find the volume in cm³.

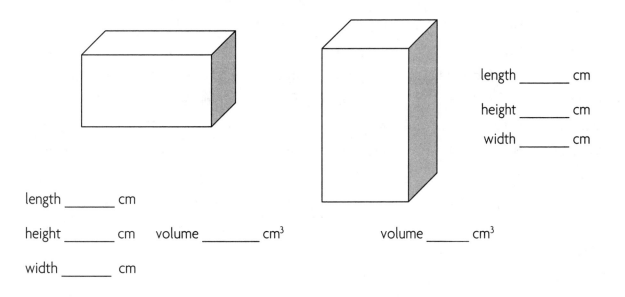

length _____ cm

height _____ cm

width _____ cm

length _____ cm

height _____ cm   volume _____ cm³

width _____ cm

volume _____ cm³

STATION 5: Determining the volume of an irregularly shaped solid

Instructions: Fill the graduated cylinder with 30 mL of water from the beaker. Tie a string to one of the irregularly shaped solids, lower it into the graduated cylinder, and record the volume. Subtract 30 mL from this volume, then convert mL to cm³ (remember, 1 mL = 1 cm³), and record the final volume. Please pour the water back into the beaker, remove the string from the irregularly shaped solid, and put these on the paper towel before leaving the station.

Item	Volume

Approximate Conversions

To Metric Measure:

inches	multiplied by 2.5*	≅	centimeters
feet	multiplied by 30	≅	centimeters
yards	multiplied by 0.9	≅	meters
miles	multiplied by 1.6	≅	kilometers
ounces	multiplied by 28	≅	grams
pounds	multiplied by 0.45	≅	kilograms
teaspoons	multiplied by 5	≅	milliliters
tablespoons	multiplied by 15	≅	milliliters
fluid ounces	multiplied by 20	≅	milliliters
cups	multiplied by 0.24	≅	liters
pints	multiplied by 0.47	≅	liters
quarts	multiplied by 0.95	≅	liters
gallons	multiplied by 3.8	≅	liters
Fahrenheit	(°F − 32) ÷ 1.8	≅	Celsius

From Metric Measure:

centimeters	multiplied by 0.4	≅	inches
meters	multiplied by 3.3	≅	feet
meters	multiplied by 1.1	≅	yards
kilometers	multiplied by 0.6	≅	miles
grams	multiplied by 0.035	≅	ounces
kilograms	multiplied by 2.2	≅	pounds
mililiters	multiplied by 0.03	≅	fluid ounces
liters	multiplied by 2.1	≅	pints
liters	multiplied by 1.06	≅	quarts
liters	multiplied by 0.26	≅	gallons
Celsius	(°C x 1.8) + 32	≅	Fahrenheit
Celsius	°C + 273.15	≅	Kelvin

Important equality of liquid volume to solid volume in metric measure: 1 mL = 1 cm³ = 1 cc

*1 inch equals 2.54 cm exactly

Measurement Standards?

Ratio of an igloo's circumference to its diameter: Eskimo Pi

2000 pounds of Chinese soup: Won ton

1 millionth of a mouthwash: 1 microScope

Time between slipping on a peel and smacking the floor: 1 bananosecond

1 million aches: 1 megahurtz

1 million microphones: 1 megaphone

10 cards: 1 decacards

10 rations: 1 decoration

2 monograms: 1 diagram

Basic unit of laryngitis: 1 hoarsepower

365.25 days of drinking diet drinks: 1 lite year

Science Class
Parent Survey

If your employment schedule permits, would you occasionally be able to come to our science classroom and serve as a lab assistant (assisting the teacher with lab set-up, lab supplies, lab cleanup, etc.)?

Do you work in a job where you must use science-related knowledge or problem-solving skills? If yes, please tell me about your job.

Would you be willing to collect household items (2-liter bottles, tissue paper, newspaper, etc.) for use in our classroom lab?

Have you ever traveled to a location where you saw naturally occurring wonders (volcanoes, geysers, marine life, etc.)? Would you be willing to come to our classroom to share your experience with us? If yes, please tell me a little bit about your experience.

Letter to Parents

Date _____

Dear Parent,

Welcome to another school year! The summers do fly by, don't they? My name is Mrs. Steward and I will be your child's science teacher this year. I have already begun to get to know my students and can tell we are going to have a great year!

As you well know, it takes a team effort to make sure your child succeeds in his or her academic efforts. I look forward to meeting you at Parent Night so we can begin our work together making sure your child gets as much out of Science class this year as he or she can!

For your information, we will be studying the following concepts this year (in roughly this order):

Semester I (Earth Science)	Semester II (Life Science)
The Solar System	Cells
Earth's Atmosphere	Classifying
Volcanoes and Earthquakes	The Plant Kingdom
The Water Cycle	The Animal Kingdom
Weather	Habitats and Environments

If you would please take a moment out of your busy schedule to fill out the attached "Parent Survey," I would really appreciate it. It is my hope to have many of you involved with our classes this year and we have many different ways you can help us!

Thanks for your time, and, please, do not hesitate to contact me if you ever have a question or concern!

Sincerely,

Sally Steward, Science Teacher
PHONE NUMBER
E-MAIL ADDRESS

Field Trip Permission Slip
(CAPITAL LETTERS indicate areas for teacher to write out.)

Today's Date_____Date Due Back to School_____

Student's Name_____

I give my child permission to attend the field trip to _____ **(LOCATION)**

on _____ **(DATE)** from _____ to _____ **(TIME**

LEAVING SCHOOL to TIME RETURNING TO SCHOOL). I understand my child will be

transported by _____ **(METHOD OF TRANSPORTATION)**.

In case of emergency during the trip, I can be reached at _____ (Please give

phone number). In the event I cannot be reached, please call _____

(Please give an emergency contact person's name, relationship to student, and phone number.)

I understand the cost of this field trip for my child is _____ **(COST PER STUDENT)**.

I ____have ____have not included that payment with this permission slip. (If payment is an issue,

please call _____ **YOUR PHONE NUMBER** to discuss other options.) I also understand

my child **WILL/WILL NOT** need to bring his/her lunch for the trip.

Parent Signature_____Date_____

Team Log for Date: _____

Those present at meeting today:

_____

Topic Discussed	Team Thoughts/Notes About This Topic	Action To Be Taken?	Responsible Person?

Substitute Lesson Plans for Date _____

● Teacher:

● Seating charts

● Attendance procedures

● Daily schedule [period, time, and room number(s)]

● Map of school

● School phone book/extension numbers

● List of people to turn to for help

● Passes procedure

● Emergency plans

● Lesson plans

● Directions for using video player, television, remote, computer, etc.

Thank you   ☺

Substitute Teacher Report Checklist

NAME _____   DATE _____

Period/Subject	Lesson Concerns or Comments	Absent Students	Student Issues (Name/Infraction)

Recipes

CORNSTARCH AND WATER MIXTURE

sometimes referred to as oobleck, from *Bartholomew and the Oobleck* by Dr. Seuss (Random House, 1976)

- 1½ c cornstarch
- 1 c water

Mix the ingredients by hand starting with all the cornstarch and about ¾ c of water until this gooey material will drip from your hand, but, when struck a glancing blow, will not splatter. If too watery, add additional cornstarch.

NOTE: Make a big serving bowl of oobleck in class with students and then ask for someone to help test it. Put the bowl in front of the seated volunteer and grab some of the oobleck and let it flow through your fingers. Inform class and participant that the test to see if oobleck is ready is to hit it hard with a fist: If it splatters, it is not ready. Then smash your fist into the mixture. Practice this several times without a "victim" so that splashes are not truly made. It is fun to watch the reaction of the participant, and, of course, all the students want to try.

SALT CRYSTALS

(kosher salt works best, but table salt can be used)

- salt
- hot water
- measuring spoons
- string
- scissors
- toothpick
- baby food or like jar

1. Attach string to toothpick. Trim string so that it will hang into jar without touching the bottom or sides. Put this apparatus to one side until ready for use.

2. Put about two tsp salt into jar.

3. Add hot water to jar until about ¾ full.

4. Stir until the salt (or most of it) dissolves.

5. Put toothpick/string apparatus into jar.

6. Let stand undisturbed for two to three days. The longer time the jar is left alone, the larger the crystals will grow.

MAGNESIUM SULFATE
(Epsom salt)

- 250 mL beaker
- measuring spoons
- scissors
- petri dish or jar lid
- magnesium sulfate
- dark colored paper
- tap water

1. Cut a circle from the dark colored paper that will fit inside the petri dish or lid.

2. Fill the beaker with water, add 4 T (60 mL) of magnesium sulfate (Epsom salt) and stir.

3. Put the dark colored paper into petri dish or lid.

4. Pour a thin layer of solution into petri dish or lid over dark colored paper.

5. Let stand undisturbed for two to three days.

SUGAR CRYSTALS

- tap water
- container for cooking
- toothpick
- sugar (save some to rub on string)
- drinking glass or the like
- string, Popsicle stick
- food coloring (optional)
- artificial flavoring (optional)

1. Boil 1 c water in a container, turn off heat, add 1 ½ c sugar, and stir. Add more sugar, if necessary, to make a saturated solution.

2. When solution cools, add color or flavoring and pour into glass.

3. Tie string to toothpick, rub sugar on string, and drop string into the solution. Allow toothpick to rest on the glass rim. If using a Popsicle stick, make a hole in one end to slide on toothpick. Leave undisturbed for several days.

CRYSTAL GARDENS

- laundry bluing
- salt (kosher works best)
- 250 mL beaker or old mixing bowl
- water
- ammonia
- porous material for crystals to grow on (sponge, bricks, lava rocks, art paper, etc.)
- food coloring (optional)

1. Add ingredients in this amount and order: 10 mL bluing (found in laundry section), 10 mL water, and 10 mL ammonia in mixing container. (If using bowl, it will probably get stained.)

2. Stir solution until salt is mostly dissolved.

3. Pour over item(s) on which crystals will grow.

4. Let stand undisturbed (may only take one day to see results).

5. If coloring, there are a couple of ways to try: add about ⅛ of small coloring bottle to solution or dab a liberal amount of coloring on growing surfaces where crystal solution was poured.

CULTURE MEDIUM

Unflavored gelatin can be used in place of agar or other culture-growing media, just follow the directions on the box and use.

FUN PUTTY

- white glue

- water

- borax (found in the laundry section of a grocery store).

Mix equal parts of white glue and water and add a borax solution (try 16 g of borax dissolved in 400 mL of warm water). Food coloring may be added (might stain your hands, though). Measure 50 mL of the glue mixture into a cup, then stir in 10 mL of borax solution. Store in a plastic bag and when it dries up, throw it away.

HYDROCHLORIC ACID

When using concentrated acid (12 M) in any of the following recipes, wear splash goggles, apron, and chemical resistant gloves. **Do not inhale the vapors!** Use a fume hood or well-ventilated area for preparation. **Immediately clean up any spillage.**

To make 1 liter of mixture:

Always add acid to water.

MOL WANTED	AMT WATER	AMT ACID
1 M	916.7 mL	83.3 mL
2 M	833.3 mL	166.7 mL
3 M	750.0 mL	250.0 mL
6 M	500.0 mL	500.0 mL

IODINE
(Tincture of Iodine)

- iodine

- methyl alcohol (burner alcohol)

Dissolve 2 g of iodine in 120 mL of alcohol. *Iodine crystals are irritating to the skin, so handle with care.*

NITRIC ACID

When using concentrated acid (15.9 M) in any of the following recipes, wear splash goggles, apron, and chemical resistant gloves. ***Do not inhale the vapors!*** Use a fume hood or well-ventilated area for preparation. ***Immediately clean up any spillage.***

To make 1 liter of mixture:

Always add acid to water.

MOL WANTED	AMT WATER	AMT ACID
1 M	937.1 mL	62.9 mL
3 M	811.3 mL	188.7 mL
6 M	622.6 mL	377.4 mL

PHENOL RED

- phenol red

- distilled water

Dissolve 1 g of phenol red in 200 mL of water. This will make a stock solution to prepare indicator solutions as needed. To use, add 4 drops of NaOH (sodium hydroxide) to 20 mL of phenol red stock solution. Add enough distilled water to make 2000 mL of phenol red indicator solution.

RED CABBAGE JUICE
(for acid/base indicator)

- red cabbage

- cooking pot

- grater

- colander (strainer)

- water

Grate the cabbage into small pieces and place them in the pot. Add water to cover cabbage. Boil until the liquid turns a dark purple color—about 20–30 minutes. Pour the liquid through a strainer to remove the cabbage, which will be a bluish/dark purple color. Test with white vinegar (an acid) and soapy water (a base). Juice should turn pink in acids and green in bases.

CAUTION: Juice will spoil in a few days even if refrigerated. Try making test paper by soaking coffee filters or filter paper with the juice and allowing it to dry.

Resources

Resources

Websites

Please note that websites are often changed, deleted, and moved.

Website   **Subject**

Chapter 1

books.nap.edu/books/
    0309053269/html/index.html .... *National Science Education Standards*,
National Academy Press, 1996, online version

Chapter 2

www.wpafb.af.mil/cap/glr-ae/lplan/oct96.htm .... survival

www.geocities.com/vishalmamania/jokes/quiz.html .... simplest quiz

www.norfacad.pvt.k12.va.us/puzzles/wacky.htm .... word pictures

www.halcyon.com/doug/ucg/kids/riddles.html .... word pictures

www.mcps.k12.md.us/schools/tildenms/Departments/
    P.E/SmithStuff/wacky_wordies.htm .... word pictures

webhome.idirect.com/~avriljohn/visual.html .... visual illusions

www.cs.brandeis.edu/~hornby/amuse/test_mental.txt .... equations test

kith.org/logos/things/sitpuz/situations.html .... situations

webusers.anet-stl.com/~kveit/me00002.htm .... posers

www.thewaitegroup.com/jokes/j54.html .... posers

www.elseroad.com/fun/intelligence/intelligence_test.htm .... posers

www.dorsai.org/~walts/iq_test.html .... posers

Chapter 3

www.weather.com .... The Weather Channel

spacelink.nasa.gov/index.html .... Spacelink resources for educators

www.nasm.edu .... National Air and Space Museum homepage

www.middleweb.com .... instructional methods and resources

www.physics4kids.com .... teacher and student information

www.biology4kids.com .... teacher and student information

www.chem4kids.com/ .... teacher and student information

school.discovery.com/lessonplans/index.html .... lesson plans

www.pacificnet.net/~mandel/index.html .... lesson plans

scifun.chem.wisc.edu/ .... lesson plans

scssi.scetv.org/cgi-bin/state/indxsrch?q_f=15 .... lesson plans

www.teach-nology.com/teachers/lesson_plans/science/basic .... lesson plans

www.exploratorium.edu .... museum site

www.project2061.org .... benchmarks search engine, other guides, ordering information

www.youth.net/nsrc .... inquiry and kit-based science education

www.ces.clemson.edu .... inquiry and kit-based science

www.si.edu/nsrc/laser/overv.htm .... inquiry and kit-based science education

einsteinproject.org .... inquiry and kit-based science education

www.jasonproject.org/ .... annual scientific expedition with live, interactive programs

earthobservatory.nasa.gov/Laboratory/ .... event-based inquiry experiments

www.pearsonlearning.com/dalesey/full_event.cfm .... event-based inquiry titles

Chapter 4

physchem.ox.ac.uk/MSDS/ .... information on MSDS sheets

www.msdssearch.com/ .... MSDS information

www.ilpi.com/msds/index.html .... MSDS information

quizhub.com/quiz/f-chemicals.cfm .... common chemical names quizzes

chemfinder.cambridgesoft.com/ .... common chemical names database

Chapter 5

rubistar.4teachers.org/ .... rubrics to create online

Chapter 6

www.seaworld.org .... animal information database

www.yahoo.com/Education/

www.infoseek.com .... good search engine for students

Chapter 7

How children learn

www.sedl.org/scimath/compass/v03n02/1.html .... best practices in science education

www.angelfire.com/oh/themidas/index.html .... best practices in science education

www.ldrc.ca/projects/miinventory/miinventory.php?
eightstyles=1 .... best practices in science education

www.ed.gov/databases/ERIC_Digests/ed410226.html .... best practices in science education

www.cudenver.edu/~mryder/itc_data/constructivism.html ...... best practices in science education

www.mcgill.ca/douglas/fdg/kjf/17-TAGLA.htm. .... best practices in science education

tip.psychology.org/bruner.html .... best practices in science education

www.mcps.k12.md.us/departments/eventscience/Origins.html .... best practices in science education

www.hardin.k12.ky.us/res_techn/grrec/webquest/
science_best_practices.htm .... best practices in science education

www.mcps.k12.md.us/departments/eii/bestpracticespg.htm .... best practices in science education

mdk12.org/practices/good_instruction/projectbetter/
science/index.html .... best practices in science education

www.exploratorium.edu/IFI/ .... best practices in science education

Lesson plan sites

www.chem4kids.com/

www.biology4kids.com/

www.geography4kids.com/ .... ecology/environment

www.physics4kids.com/

school.discovery.com/lessonplans/index.html

www.opticalres.com/kidoptx.html

www.brainpop.com/

www.physicalscienceseries.com/programs.htm

scifun.chem.wisc.edu/

www.energyquest.ca.gov/index.html

Demonstrations

www.sciencenetlinks.com/matrix.cfm .... teacher demonstrations for safety

scied.unl.edu/pages/mamres/pages/demos/demo.html .... science demonstrations

scied.unl.edu/pages/mamres/pages/demos/physical/physical.htm .. science demonstrations

scied.unl.edu/pages/sciencedemos/index.htm .... science demonstrations

www.itg.lbl.gov/ITG.hm.pg.docs/dissect/info.html .... virtual frog dissection

www.epa.gov/region7/education_resources/teachers/
    ehsstudy/ehs12.htm .... suggestions and additional sites for chemical
                                                                                 alternatives

www.thecatalyst.org/hwrp/safetymanual/earth_space_concerns.html

Science kit retailers other than school science catalogs

www.einsteins-emporium.com/

www.discoverthis.com/

www.terrifictoy.com/

www.thinkertoyscarmel.com/

www.pishtoys.com/index.html

Chapter 11

www.schoolgrants.org .... grants clearinghouse and tips for grant-writing

www.eschoolnews.com/resources/funding .... daily grant and funding sources

www.ed.gov/topics/topics.jsp?&top=Grants+%26+Contracts .... U.S. Department of Education site for federal
                                                                                 funding opportunities

Print References and Resources

Chapter 1
Reference

National Research Council. 1996. *National science education standards*. Washington, DC: National Academy Press. Online version at: *www.nap.edu/books/0309053269/html/index.html*

Book/Print Resources

American Association for the Advancement of Science (AAAS) and National Science Teachers Association (NSTA). 2001. *Atlas of science literacy (Project 2061)*. Washington, DC: AAAS and NSTA. ISBN# 0-87168-668-6

American Association for the Advancement of Science (AAAS). 1993. *Benchmarks for science literacy (Project 2061)*. Washington, DC: AAAS. ISBN# 0-19-508986-3

National Research Council. 1996. *National science education standards*. Washington, DC: National Academy Press. Online version at: *www.nap.edu/books/0309053269/html/index.html*

Chapter 3
References

American Association for the Advancement of Science (AAAS) and National Science Teachers Association (NSTA). 2001. *Atlas of science literacy (Project 2061)*. Washington, DC: AAAS and NSTA. ISBN# 0-87168-668-6

Center for Early Adolescence. 1985. *Seven developmental needs of young adolescents*. Carrboro, NC: University of North Carolina at Chapel Hill.

Colburn, A. 2000. An inquiry primer. *Science Scope* 23 (6): 42–44.

Ediger, M. 2001. A project method in middle school science. *IN Focus* 30 (Summer): 17–19.

Holliday, W. 2001a. Modeling in science. *Science Scope* 25 (2): 56–59.

Holliday, W. 2001b. Scaffolding in science. *Science Scope* 25 (1): 68–71.

Book/Print Resources

American Association for the Advancement of Science (AAAS) and National Science Teachers Association (NSTA). 2001. *Atlas of science literacy (Project 2061)*. Washington, DC: AAAS and NSTA. ISBN# 0-87168-668-6

American Association for the Advancement of Science (AAAS). 1993. *Benchmarks for science literacy (Project 2061)*. Washington, DC: AAAS. ISBN# 0-19-508986-3

Center for Early Adolescence. 1985. *Seven developmental needs of young adolescents*. Carrboro, NC: University of North Carolina at Chapel Hill.

Connors, N. A. 2000. *If you don't feed the teachers they eat the students! Guide to success for administrators and teachers*. Nashville, TN: Incentive Publications, Inc. ISBN# 0-86530-457-2 (humorous advice for educators)

Irvin, J. L., ed. 1992. *Transforming middle level education: Perspectives and possibilities*. Boston: Allyn & Bacon. ISBN# 0-205-13472-6

Rutherford, F. J., and A. Ahlgren. 1990. *Science for all Americans*. New York: Oxford Press. ISBN# 0-19-506771-1

Schurr, S. L. 1998. *Dynamite in the classroom: A how-to handbook for teachers*. Westerville, OH: NMSA Publications. ISBN# 1-56090-044-5 (middle grades instructional methods)

Wormeli, R. 2001. *Meet me in the middle*. Westerville, OH: Stenhouse Publishers in conjunction with the National Middle School Association. ISBN# 1-57110-328-7 (middle grades instructional methods)

Chapter 4
Book/Print Resource

Kwan, T., and J. Texley. In press. *Inquiring safely: A guide for middle school teachers*. Arlington, VA: NSTA Press.

Chapter 5
References

Center for Early Adolescence. 1985. *Seven developmental needs of young adolescents*. Carrboro, NC: University of North Carolina at Chapel Hill.

Johnson, D. W., R. T. Johnson, and E. J. Holubec. 1994. *The new circles of learning: Cooperation in the classroom and school*. Alexandria, VA: Association for Supervision and Curriculum Development.

Lanzoni, M. 1997. *A middle school teacher's guide to cooperative learning*. Topsfield, MA: New England League of Middle Schools.

Wood, K. 1992. Meeting the needs of young adolescents through cooperative learning. In *Transforming middle level education*, ed., J. L. Irvin. 314–335. Boston: Allyn & Bacon.

Chapter 7
References

Farenga, S. J., B. A. Joyce, and T. W. Dowling. 2002. Rocketing into adaptive inquiry. *Science Scope* 25 (4): 34–39.

Colburn, A. 2000. An inquiry primer. *Science Scope* 23 (6): 42–44.

National Science Teachers Association (NSTA) Board of Directors. Adopted in January 1990. *NSTA Position Statement*. NSTA Committees and Task Forces. Retrieved January 29, 2002, from *www.nsta.org/ 159&psid=16*

Book/Print Resources

Sarquis, M., and J. Sarquis. 1991. *Fun with chemistry*. Madison, WI: Institute for Chemical Education (ICE Publication 91-005). (labs and activities plus an appendix with a list of chemicals, common names, and where these can be purchased)

Chapter 10
Reference

Wong, H. K., and R. T. Wong. 1998. *The first days of school: How to be an effective teacher*. Mountain View, CA: Harry K. Wong Publications.

Book/Print Resources

Center for Early Adolescence. 1985. *Seven developmental needs of young adolescents*. Carrboro, NC: University of North Carolina at Chapel Hill.

Stevenson, C. 1998. *Teaching ten to fourteen year olds*. New York: Longman/Allyn & Bacon. ISBN #0-0813-1582-4 (middle grades teaching textbook)

Chapter 12
Reference

Arnold, J., and C. Stevenson. 1998. *Teachers' teaming handbook: A middle level planning guide*. Fort Worth, TX: Harcourt Brace College Publishers.

Book/Print Resources

Forte, I., and S. Schurr. 1996. *Integrating instruction in science: Strategies, activities, projects, tools, & techniques*. Nashville, TN: Incentive Publications, Inc. ISBN# 0-86530-321-5 (activities, projects, and integration techniques)

Rottier, J. 2001. *Implementing and improving teaming*. Westerville, OH: NMSA Publications. ISBN# 156090-166-7 (teaming handbook for middle grades teachers)

Chapter 14
Book/Print Resource

National Research Council. 1996. *National science education standards*. Washington, DC: National Academy Press. Online version at: *www.nap.edu/books/ 0309053269/html/index.html*

Professional Associations
Chapter 11

National Science Teachers Association (*www.nsta.org*) 1840 Wilson Boulevard, Arlington, VA 22201-3000 703-243-7100

National Middle School Association (*www.nmsa.org*) 4151 Executive Parkway, Suite 300, Westerville, OH 43081 1-800-528-NMSA

Periodicals
Chapter 2

Games Magazine, PO Box 2055, Marion, OH 43306-8155 (puzzles and games)

World of Puzzles (by Games Magazine), PO Box 2032, Marion, OH 43306-8132 (puzzles and games)

Chapter 11

Science Scope, a journal for middle and junior high school science teachers, available through the National Science Teachers Association by becoming an NSTA member. (NSTA, 1840 Wilson Boulevard, Arlington, VA 22201-3000, 703-243-7100. *www.nsta.org*)

Chapter 12

Science Scope, a journal for middle and junior high school science teachers, available through the National Science Teachers Association by becoming an NSTA member. (NSTA, 1840 Wilson Boulevard, Arlington, VA 22201-3000, 703-243-7100. *www.nsta.org*)

Science Supply Companies
Chapter 4

Many of these companies offer kit-based science resources. Chemicals purchased from many of these companies will include the MSDS.

AIMS Education Foundation, PO Box 8120, Fresno, CA 93747-8120 1-888-733-2467 (*www.AIMSedu.com*)

Carolina Biological Supply, 2700 York Road, Burlington, NC 27215 1-800-334-5551 (*www.carolina.com*)

Flinn Scientific, Inc., PO Box 219, Batavia, IL 60510 1-800-452-1261 (*www.flinnsci.com*) This company catalog lists chemical storage and removal guidelines.

Frey Scientific, 100 Paragon Parkway, PO Box 8108, Mansfield, OH 44903 1-800-225-FREY (*www.freyscientific.com*)

Nasco, 901 Janesville Ave., PO Box 901, Fort Atkinson
WI 53538-0901
1-800-558-9595 (*www.eNASCO.com*)
Pitsco, Inc. PO Box 1708, Pittsburg, KS 66762 1-800-
358-4983 (*www.shop-pitsco.com*)
Sargent-Welch/Cenco, PO Box 5229, Buffalo Grove,
IL 60089-5229
1-800-727-4368 (*www.sargentwelch.com*)
Science Kit & Boreal Laboratories, 777 East Park Drive,
PO Box 5003, Tonawanda, NY 14151-5003
1-800-828-7777 (*www.sciencekit.com*)

These companies sell small toys and other items that
can be used in hands-on activities:

Oriental Trading Company, Inc., PO Box 2308, Omaha,
NE 68103-2308 (*www.orientaltradingcompany.com*)
US Toys Co., Inc., 13210 Arrington Road, Grandview,
MO 64030-2886
Mindware, 121 5th Avenue NW, New Brighton, MN
55112 (*www.mindwareonline.com*)

Index